The Darkness Is Not Dark

Overcoming Guillain-Barré Syndrome

Regina R. Roth

*A wife's diary of steadfast love, lighthearted hope, and abiding
faith throughout the duration of her husband's debilitating disease*

The Darkness Is Not Dark
by Regina R. Roth

Printed in the United States of America

ISBN 1-59467-109-5

Fruit-Bearer Publishing
A Branch of Candy's Creations
P.O. Box 777, Georgetown, DE 19947
(302) 856-6649 • Fax (302) 856-7742
fruitbearer.publishing@verizon.net
www.fruitbearer.com
Graphic design and cover by Candy Abbott

www.xulonpress.com

Whither shall I go from thy Spirit? Or whither shall I flee from thy Presence?

If I ascend to heaven, thou art there! If I make my bed in Sheol, thou art there!

If I take the wings of the morning and dwell in the uttermost parts of the sea, even there thy hand shall lead me, and thy right hand shall hold me! If I say, "Let only darkness cover me, and the light about me be night," even the darkness is not dark to thee, the night is bright as the day; for darkness is as light with thee.

— Psalm 139: 7-12 (RSV)

Dedication

This book is dedicated to our granddaughters, Jesse Marie, Emily Rae, Rebekah Rae, Madeline Grace, Sarah Grace, and any grandchildren yet to be born. May you always know how deep my love for each of you is and how even deeper is God's love for you and for all of us. I also dedicate this book to our children and sons-in-law, Karen, Sherry, Chad, Dennis, and Tom who suffered with us, held our hands, and cheered us on. All our extended family and friends who prayed for us and shared their time and talents deserve very special thanks, for which no words are adequate. The extensive cast of medical personnel from doctors and therapists to overworked nurses, aides, and assistants deserve much praise and many thanks for their excellent care.

And, to my husband Roland, whose suffering, courage, "never-give-up" attitude, and love taught all of us the importance of family and community and deepened our respect for the fragility and sacredness of life—Thank You.

Acknowledgments

I would like to acknowledge and thank my friend Candy Abbott of Fruit-Bearer Publishing who encouraged and assisted me in bringing this diary into print. Candy, my family, and friends convinced me that, in this sharing of a difficult life event, others might become aware of the truth of God's promise of faithfulness and love in the good times *and* the difficult times of their lives.

And thanks to Pastor Skip Keels, who has preached over and over how we need to share with others our stories of God's love and grace for us all. As a shy, private person I was hesitant to do this. I intend for these words to be God's words, not mine.

Introduction

This is my story of our family's journey through the debilitating and far-reaching effects of the illness, Guillain-Barré Syndrome (GBS). My husband contracted GBS September 1, 1999. We are still in recovery. One purpose in sharing my diary is to increase knowledge about this hideous illness. Few people have heard of it or know anyone who has been stricken by it. I hope to increase awareness so that a quick and proper diagnosis might be possible for future victims.

My story, however, is from the heart and will be skimpy on complicated, confusing medical details. My second and chief purpose in sharing our story is to demonstrate God's faithfulness in dark days and the important value in community of family, friends, and even strangers. Many parts of this story are painful to recall. Some parts are very personal and difficult to share. However, I hope the times of joy, encouragement, and thankfulness will be obvious. There *is* a balm in Gilead. (Jeremiah 8: 22; American Folk Hymn, *The Methodist Hymnal*.)

Unfortunately, pain and sorrow come to all of us at some time or another (maybe several times) in this life. I do not in any way purport our suffering to be worse than anyone else's agonies. I simply hope our experience may be a type of hand holding to all who are walking through a dark valley of life right now or will do so in the future.

I do not believe that God inflicts hardships upon His children to teach them a lesson or for any other reason. That, to my mind, would not be actions of a God of undying, caring love, which is how I view God. I believe God loves us through all of life's events—the good, the bad, and the ugly.

The world is full of tragedies, unfairness, and strife. We are bombarded daily via newspapers and television with stories of some of life's most horrible tragedies and pain. Sometimes these events touch our lives personally. The temptation is to extend our hands heavenward and cry out, *"Why, why, why, oh God?"* Of course, I do not have any "pat" answers, and I do not claim to understand life's many sad, as well as joyous, mysteries. The only thing I am sure of is that God walks alongside us in all our joy and in all our sorrow. In our grief and anguish it can be easy to ignore God's love and say, *"Where is God now?"* I believe that trust, when everything is crashing down around us, is necessary. We must open our hearts and allow Him to enter and to walk the dark valley with us.

These words of belief are easy to write and speak. The hard part is continuing to believe and have faith in God when the living of very painful days is excruciating. I have found God's promises to be true. When God has seemed absent in my life, I have realized it is because I thought I could do everything by myself. Or, I wondered how could God care about and even be aware of little ol' me. Or, I asked how could God let this happen. I can be hardheaded and blind at times, but the experience you will read about in the pages ahead opened my eyes and turned all doubts into a deeper and more grateful faith than I had previously experienced. I don't have all the answers. My spiritual journey continues, and I hope my story will encourage and inspire you wherever you are in your spiritual journey. I am confident God will meet you wherever you are right now. God's grace is given freely to all of us unconditionally. Thanks and praise for such a wonderful gift!

Regina R. Roth
July 2005

Foreword

by Adam Porter
Reprinted with permission from an article published in the September 22,
2000, *THE REVIEW*, the student newspaper at the University of Delaware

It was the first of September 1999, a Wednesday, and classes had just
begun at the University of Delaware.

That afternoon, Professor Roland Roth was speaking to his mammalogy
lab students in Townsend Hall when he began to notice a slight numbness
in the index finger of his right hand. Quickly brushing it off, he continued
his animated lecturing, slowly pacing in front of the class.

Soon, he noticed that another fingertip had gone numb.

By 5:30 p.m., Roth had lost feeling in three of the fingers on his
right hand, as well as his toes and the bottoms of his feet. Although
this seemed odd, he had never been one to make a big deal out of
something "insignificant"—so he finished the lab and went home.

Five days later, an alarmed group of Christiana Care staff members
crowded around Roth's body attempting to resuscitate him. It was a
Code Blue emergency. His heart had stopped beating.

"They picked me up and put me on the bed, and the next thing I
knew, I had a mask over my mouth and someone said, 'Okay, he has
a pulse,'" Roth says, sitting back and laughing. "I was never able to do

anything like sitting up again until October."

After enduring [two] weeks of rapidly declining muscle control, Roth's condition leveled off, and the recovery process began.

Roth is a victim of Guillain-Barré Syndrome, a rare disorder involving loss of muscle control and paralysis due to nerve tissue degradation.

For some victims of the syndrome—which affects eight in every 100,000 people—the ordeal is over in two or three months, and complete bodily control is reestablished. Roth was not so fortunate.

Due to severe nerve damage, his recovery process slowly continues today after almost a year of rehab.

Guillain-Barré, which usually follows a minor infection, occurs after the antibodies mistake nerve tissue for invading proteins. In essence, the body destroys its own control network.

Recollecting his steep decline over those first few weeks in September, his daughter Karen says her father's systems shut down little by little.

"It was literally almost each hour that you could see him getting worse," she says. "He couldn't walk, then he couldn't sit up, then he couldn't feed himself, and he would choke on food because he couldn't swallow. Finally, we would have to tape his eyes shut because he couldn't close them to rest."

Roth's doctors couldn't offer him much encouraging information. They gave him pheresis treatments, which consist of filtering blood to remove antibodies, as well as adding synthetic plasma. Roth endured the four-hour procedure five times, although there was no way to determine to what extent it helped him.

After having a tube down his throat for a time, doctors wanted to perform a tracheotomy. The incision in his throat would allow a new breathing tube an entryway.

"If they said I needed a tracheotomy, well then go for it, baby, if it means I can breathe without this thing down my throat," Roth says, smiling. And he always tried to show a smile.

"The hardest part of this disease is that the doctors say, 'It's going to get worse before it gets better,'" Karen says, remembering the arduous wait for a sign of improvement.

"It continued to surprise us every day at how wicked it was and how it robbed him of something every day," says Roth's wife Regina. In a family of firm supporters, Regina was the strongest.

"From September till I came home from rehab, she was out there virtually every day," Roth says in a deep, affectionate tone.

Regina spent day and night by her husband's side, especially in those first few weeks. However, there was one exception. On September 15, 1999, the day of Hurricane Floyd—the day Roth began hallucinating. Regina was not able to be with her husband because of the severe weather conditions, which seemed to correspond with his declining health. For the week and a half prior, Roth had been getting little sleep, mainly due to discomfort.

"Think about it tonight," he says. "When you go to bed, don't move after you get in your bed. And then think, well I'd like my arm over here. So you have to ask someone to move it for you."

An independent individual, Roth admits that his strong suit was not asking people to do things for him.

As his son Chad recalls, "He would say, 'Chad, I hate to bother you, but I need my hands readjusted.'"

As the exhaustion from lack of sleep accumulated, Roth says his mind began to fatigue. "I believed I was suspended on the wall, so I always thought that I was in danger of falling. The ceiling became the wall opposite me, so you can imagine the dimensions of the room," Roth says about his most vivid hallucination.

"I kept feeling like plastic cleaner bags were wound around my arms and legs, which kept me on the bed. Then there were spider webs floating across my vision."

At this point, the family became truly scared. The doctors had never said anything about the effects the syndrome would have on the mind of their loved one.

"The day they moved him to the ICU, he said that he saw eagles flying around the room," Karen recalls. "He was yelling at us and telling us to leave the room. He was completely out of his head."

Shortly after, Roth was put on a respirator, with a tube forced down his throat providing oxygen. He slept for two days straight.

"You see this man that was just teaching classes two weeks before, and now he is unable to move, unable to breathe, unable to speak, and it's just his own body doing this to him," Karen says. "The figure that was always my rock is now totally dependent on me and my family."

Eventually, things began to improve, and in the beginning of October, the Roth family watched as their husband and father entered rehab, taking his first steps on the long road to recovery.

Roth has progressed amazingly since his early days of rehab. His recent accomplishments include walking up a flight of stairs with only one hand on the rail and doing assisted squats.

While Roth serves as an inspiration for the family, their devotion and support are what keeps him positive.

"I think the best thing you can have is a good support group," Roth says.

Prologue

Today—September 1, 1999—a little red, 3 x 5", 80-page notebook rests at the bottom of my pocketbook. This little notebook is usually neglected except to provide paper for short shopping lists or paper in which to wrap overchewed gum. It has no idea today that it will soon be filled with words of pain, suffering, confusion, and fear. It will also be used for descriptions of great joy, hope, love, and friendship. Most of all, the little red notebook will become a home for praise to God for His steadfast and never-ending love and guidance. Thank you, Little Red Notebook, for becoming my friend on this journey that is about to begin. You are now more than a little red notebook. You have become . . .

The Diary

Wednesday, September 1, 1999

When Roland came home from teaching his first day of fall semester classes at the University of Delaware, he reported, in a puzzled tone, that during his mammalogy lab he began to feel numbness in his left, and then his right, index fingers. Other fingers felt a bit strange, and his feet began to feel as though they "had Novocain in them."

How odd, we thought and wondered: *What is going on? Oh well, it will pass.* Roland had been troubled all summer by occasional diarrhea but never got around to seeing a doctor about it, dismissing it as a side effect of a prescription. It got better on its own, so we were not very concerned about these new happenings.

The evening is routine—dinner, watching the news, and Roland retreating to his downstairs office to prepare for the next day's classes and meetings.

Thursday, September 2, 1999

This morning Roland noticed that fingers on both hands are numb and tingly. Feet still feel numb as well. He called the doctor's office and was told to go to the emergency room to get it checked out.

He said his whole left side is feeling weak too. Could this be a stroke?

First, though, Roland felt obliged to go to the office and get a colleague to hold the first meeting today of his New Student Seminar—a once-a-week class. He wanted to be sure the students received all of the first-day handouts and be prepared for next week's class, when Roland would return. He also e-mailed his mammalogy students to cancel class at 2 p.m. He would see them next Tuesday.

3:30 p.m. We spent the rest of this day in the emergency room getting checked out. Stroke was ruled out. Roland was told to make an appointment with a neurologist. He did—for September 16.

During the long wait in the emergency room, an orderly who had just transferred a patient asked me why I was there. I told him briefly that I really didn't know what was wrong with my husband. He wished me luck and said he would pray for us. I thought that probably wouldn't be necessary but thanked him anyway.

Now as I review my diary, I have a new perspective on prayer and its true power and blessing in our lives. Little did I know at the time how much we needed this man's prayer! How much we *think* we know and control and how quickly we can find how much we don't know nor have control over.

Tonight we went on a short neighborhood walk, and Roland took along a cane for extra support. He noticed he couldn't rise up on his toes. This day was not what we planned.

Friday, September 3, 1999

Roland didn't feel good—still numb and weak. He called the neurologist's office early in the morning, explained the symptoms, and requested that the doctor call him back.

No response from the doctor all day. At 6:00 p.m. Roland called again. The doctor on duty told him that since the symptoms had spread, Roland should go to the emergency room. *Again?*

I suggested that maybe we should wait and see how he's feeling tomorrow or even after the weekend. After all, it *is* Labor Day weekend, and you know how crowded and hectic the emergency room will be! Fortunately, Roland vetoed this suggestion, and we returned to the emergency room. I drove—an unusual arrangement for us for evening driving. I did not know this new arrangement would last a long time.

Roland walked into the hospital carefully but on his own. After another evaluation by the neurologist, including a spinal tap, Guillain-Barré is the diagnosis. What is that? What does this mean? How soon can we get out of here? What lies ahead? I'm afraid! The doctor kindly tells us that things will probably get very bad but will likely return to normal or near normal. We need and want to know more but are too tired and bewildered to ask many questions. I finally leave Roland in the emergency room at 1:00 a.m. and go home in tears, alone.

My nightly prayer is a jumble of frantic pleas to God. Roland is afraid, too, I think, but is acting brave. He gets moved to a room by 3:30 a.m. I called our daughter Karen who lives nearby and alerted her that I think we're in for something bad, but I'm not sure what. She phones our daughter Sherry, who lives in Madison, Wisconsin, and our son Chad, living near San Francisco, California.

Saturday, September 4, 1999

I woke up early, unrested and agitated. All I can pray is, "God, please see us through this day." I head to the hospital and find Roland in Room 5212. He is trying to eat breakfast and is having trouble holding his fork. It looks awkward in his hand. When he tries to get out of bed to go to the bathroom, his legs are weak and bowed out. The nurse must assist him and then help him back into bed. Is this the same person who three days ago was a fast-moving, full-of-energy, dynamic man? Oh, Guillain-Barré, how much are you going to take away from us? What *is* this GBS thing anyway?

A three-and-a-half hour procedure called "Plasmapheresis" was given to Roland in the afternoon. In layman's terms, this procedure removes the blood from his body, extracts the plasma and the misbehaving antibodies in it, and transfuses synthetic plasma with blood cells back into his body.

Doctors' explanations of GBS have been technical and somewhat vague. This is how I understand what it is, in probably oversimplified language. A person's antibodies detect a foreign protein in the body (a virus or bacterium perhaps?) and begin their job of attacking to rid the body of it. Something unknown goes wrong, and the antibodies go too far in their defense and attack the myelin sheath of the nerve cells, destroying them. In some cases the rampage continues on into the center of the nerves—the axon, also destroying it. Then muscles cannot receive their directions for movement from the nervous system. The progression of this muscle loss usually is from one's extremities (fingers and toes) inward toward the trunk of the body and upward. The severity of the attack varies widely among victims. Some may experience paralysis only below the waist; others only from the waist up. Some have mild cases with paralysis lasting only a short while. In most cases, the antibody attack runs its course, the paralysis stabilizes, the nerves begin to slowly heal, and ability to move gradually returns. Hence, this is what the doctor meant when he said the progression is downhill, plateau, and then pulling up out of it. Some patients experience total loss of bodily movement up through the entire body to the eyes including losing the ability to breathe on one's own. Of course, we are hoping Roland's case will be of the mild variety and that he will get out of the hospital so we can soon get back to our usual lives. [We later learned that GBS can strike victims more than once—very rare, but it has happened.]

Sunday, September 5, 1999

Roland's muscles are totally useless. He cannot lift his arms or hands. He cannot scratch his nose. He cannot sit alone, much less stand or walk. It takes three strong people to get him from the bed onto the bedside toilet. The bowel muscles are failing, too. He cannot get comfortable and complains his lips and face feel "funny."

We have had some visitors. Sherry and Chad are flying in tonight and tomorrow. We need our family and friends as never before. The nurses are wonderful and are trying to do all they can to make Roland comfortable. Sometimes I am so frightened as I see him decline that I forget to lean on God. I hope others are praying for us.

I feel entirely helpless. I can't take care of this nor can I fix it. We are completely in the hands of the medical professionals and must trust in their knowledge and skills. I believe, too, that we are in God's hands and have to trust in His grace and mercy.

Monday, September 6, 1999—Labor Day

Roland reports he had to yell for nurses during the night since he cannot push the call button. His back and neck are hurting, and Tylenol with codeine has been given. I fed him his breakfast. Chad has arrived and is giving Roland massages. Roland is worried about his classes. Karen (an administrator in Roland's college) is working on arrangements for coverage.

Pheresis took five hours to complete today leaving Roland weak and exhausted. Chad left to get pizza. Roland wanted to try to sit on the bedside toilet, so four nurses lugged him onto it. I was talking on the phone when suddenly Roland slumped forward and "Code Blue" was blaring from loudspeakers outside the room. A nurse rushed in telling me to leave quickly. As I left the room, doctors and medical personnel were running toward our room. The Code Blue was for Roland. I stared in tearful horror at the action going on inside 5212 to save my husband's life. Karen and I hung onto each other as Chad reappeared with a now unwanted pizza. We all cried in shock and disbelief. Soon, a nurse came to us and said, "All is well. He's on oxygen and is okay." *Thank you, God! Thank you, fast, efficient hospital personnel!*

After giving Roland small bits of turkey, dressing, and Jell-O, brushing his teeth, and settling him in the bed, we all headed for home about 8:00 p.m., exhausted, frightened, and grateful.

The neurologist who never called us back Friday stopped in to check on Roland. He predicted Roland would be here a week and then could go to rehab. I resisted telling him how upset I am that he never called us back on Friday! Another doctor is now handling Roland's case. I'm thinking that if the doctor had returned Roland's call early Friday, medical attention might have started sooner, which could be important here. If GBS had been suspected when we first came to the ER on Thursday, might there be a difference in Roland's eventual outcome? We'll never know. [We now understand that no available test could have quickly confirmed GBS on Thursday. However, some doctors can recognize suspicious symptoms early while other doctors are very late in ever considering the possibility of GBS. The confirming sign, the presence of certain proteins in the spinal fluid, requires time to appear. Detection involves doing a spinal tap, which carries some risks. It is therefore not one of the tests doctors resort to using immediately, for obvious reasons.]

Tuesday, September 7, 1999

Sherry, Chad, and I arrive about 8:00 a.m. Overnight, a catheter was put in, which Roland doesn't like. He's still on oxygen and is eating more slowly. Sherry, with graduate degrees in biology and ecology, is going to teach Roland's class this afternoon. Karen will introduce her, and Chad says he will be the "enforcer." Roland gave them a few pointers. A kidney specialist put a shunt in Roland's groin to ease the pheresis process. Roland is beginning to report seeing strange images when his eyes are closed. Two friends arrived to feed Roland his dinner. Another friend arrived later, and all three helped stretch Roland's arms. A friend graciously invited me to dinner at Chili's. It was good, I guess, to get away from the hospital a bit, but I felt guilty. I wanted to eat quickly and get back to Roland. Home by 9:30 tonight.

Wednesday, September 8, 1999

We've had many calls both at home and at the hospital as well as many visitors. *Thank you, God, for all these wonderful people for being here with us. Thank you, God, for all those people all over the country who are praying for us.* We have received many beautiful flowers as well.

The speech and swallowing therapist checked Roland's swallowing ability and changed his diet to all soft foods. He keeps requesting more and more pillows as he tries to get comfortable. Apparently, he had a rough night last night and stretched the nurses' patience. Roland reports that after numerous attempts to get him comfortable, one nurse finally said, "Mr. Roth, we can't keep doing this. Just be quiet and go to sleep." Of course, Roland, they don't have time to stand around fluffing and re-fluffing your pillows! If you could just see how busy they are and how much they are already doing for you, you would be more understanding.

At home, two of our basement walls are torn out for new footings and foundation to be put in. Bad timing! But this was already underway before Roland became ill. I hope it doesn't get on my already frayed nerves too much.

Thursday, September 9, 1999

Physical deterioration continues. Still no bowel movement. Increase in throat phlegm. Right shoulder painful. Can't get into a comfortable position. We constantly readjust him. Many friends here to try to help him get food down. More beautiful flowers from friends as well. Our kids in and out all day. I went to dinner with friends just across the road from the hospital. I went through the motions of eating, but my eyes, my mind, my heart were turned toward the hospital. How can I enjoy myself when he is across the way suffering so? Guilt enveloped me, and I could hardly wait to return to his side.

Friday, September 10, 1999

Roland was given an EMG test today to detect how much nerve damage has occurred at this point. Still no bowel movement. Guess the muscles needed for that are shutting down. Pheresis treatment again today. His voice is weaker and the left side of his mouth droopy. He says it feels like heavy weights are on his feet and knees when nothing is there but a light sheet.

A new roommate arrived and was immediately visited by many noisy people. Fortunately, Roland was moved to a private room by evening. Sherry is spending the night at Roland's bedside.

At home, tired and dejected, I tried to do some needed housecleaning. Why? I wonder. Having a clean house is suddenly not really all that important. I think the important things in my life are becoming clearer, and the dust rag and vacuum cleaner just got lower on the list.

Saturday, September 11, 1999

A pretty good night last night. Roland is having some hallucinations. Are they being caused by the pain killing and relaxation medicines? Good bowel action today finally; first in a week. More phlegm now in throat so he needs more suctioning. Mouth still droopy and cannot close his left eye. More hallucinations throughout the day. Doctor now giving medication to try to stop them. Chad brought in new high top sneakers to give ankle support and to prevent foot drop. Chad shaved him and posted a sketch of Roland the "Bird Man" outside the door so visitors can find this room. (Roland teaches bird courses and does research on the Wood Thrush). Dennis (Karen's husband) will spend the night trying to keep Roland comfortable—Good luck, Dennis!

Friends took me to eat at a restaurant near the hospital. I could see Roland's lighted room from where I was seated. My throat closed, the tears flowed, and I could barely eat while looking up at his room, knowing he was lying helplessly there and getting worse by the minute.

I couldn't wait to get back to his bedside. How could I enjoy dinner when he couldn't even hold a fork or swallow? Fear and sadness overwhelmed me. I've always loved eating out. Tonight it held no charm. The food was tasteless and caught in my throat. People all around me were laughing and gorging on large servings of food—probably oblivious to how fortunate they were to just be able to swallow and to taste, to have family and friends with them to enjoy a meal and just be together. Part of me wanted to get up and run out, and part of me wanted to stand up and shout, "Wake up, people! Look at all you have and all you are able to do! You can chew your food and swallow it! You can laugh and talk with your family and friends! You can get up out of your chair and walk out of here! You can scratch your head if it itches! It can all vanish in a flash! Wake up! Live every moment in gratefulness for this miracle we have called LIFE!" But of course I didn't want to create a spectacle, so I put down my fork and choked back the tears.

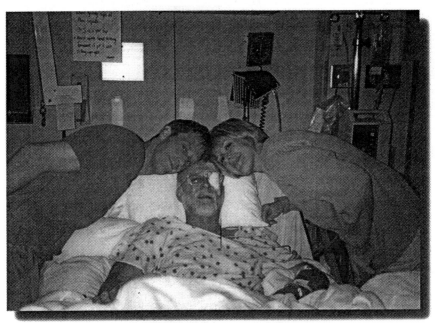

Chad and Karen with Roland as Guillain-Barré takes him on a on downhill slide

Sunday, September 12, 1999

Dennis was relieved, after a hard night, by Chad at 7:00 a.m. Roland wanted Dennis to read Ecclesiastes to him so maybe he could fall asleep. Dennis fell asleep instead!

Roland keeps asking us what he's holding in his hands; nothing is there. He can't believe it. Last pheresis treatment began at 11:30 a.m. and lasted 4 hours. Blood pressure 192/94. Nauseated, so IV fluids started. Voice very weak; doesn't want to talk to visitors. We constantly reposition him to try to make him more comfortable. No position is comfortable for more than a few seconds. Sherry left at 3: 15 p.m. to return to Wisconsin—a hard goodbye for everyone.

Roland keeps asking if he can have some gum to chew and why can't he get up on hands and knees to stretch. Chad has overnight duty tonight.

Monday, September 13, 1999

Chad was awake all night as was Roland. Roland couldn't get comfortable, talked gibberish, and continued feeling phantom objects in his hands. A friend came in to feed Roland breakfast and fainted during it—a brief diversion of which Roland was aware and about which we laughed in hindsight! Roland's vital lung capacity is falling. He reports again feeling objects between his fingers, thinks his hands are moving when not, and feels his body moving forward and backward. Tough time swallowing. Tongue out of control. A syringe is being used for liquids; pills crushed into the applesauce. He is so uncomfortable and weary. I pray to God to please give Chad strength AND patience as he is to spend the night again.

Tuesday, September 14, 1999

Chad left exhausted after another sleepless night of trying to make Roland comfortable and listening to his crazy talk. A nurse and I worked for a solid hour with 18 pillows and folded or rolled towels to try to help him get comfortable—to no avail. Here is a list of his sensations and hallucinations:

Feels like he's holding a cup of coffee

Thinks the ceiling is the far wall and the wall is the ceiling so feels that he is hanging on the near wall

Feels like he's in a dollhouse

Sees daylight through the ceiling from the floor above and shadows
of persons walking up there

Heard a dog barking, a radio, and someone clapping

Room is tilted sideways

Thinks he's in a knapsack hanging on the wall

Sees things flying around the room

Forgets he's a patient—says he's going to go to the restroom

Asks when can he go to sleep

Feels pins, sticks, and scotch tape between his fingers

By afternoon, the doctor decides it's time to move him to Intensive
Care. I followed the gurney as we moved him through the hospital to
ICU, listening to him jabbering on like a crazy person spiraling down,
down, down into an unknown abyss. When will he hit bottom? And
how much worse can this get? *God, please prop us up; we're sliding
down the slippery slope of despair.*

Wednesday, September 15, 1999

Rain began falling today. And so did we—into despair. Hallucinations
dominated this long day. Roland thinks he has moved to another room.
He told me in a weak but agitated voice about the whole ICU going on
a field trip to a boat docked somewhere in lower Delaware, and he fell
into a hole in a restaurant. They also visited a duck lodge. Told me he is
just one of a group of people from church with this disease. "We'll fix
it!" Here are more of his babbling comments all uttered in a panicked,
frantic, or angry voice:

"Throw these sunglass frames away so I won't see them."

"I was wrapped in blankets with my head on a cash register."

"Get those glasses out of my hands again and throw them away!
Oh, wait, they are good and should go to the Lion's Club."

"There's a wheel in my crotch. I need to stand up to see what's
there."

"Throw that away! I already asked Chad to throw it away."

"This is a hospital bed? You didn't tell me that! I thought it was our bedroom bed."

"So, I can't get up and run out of here? Because I'm attached to a tube?"

"Get these glasses out of my hand again!"

"How am I supposed to get out of here?"

"I'm not under house arrest!"

"Are these gold cobwebs floating in here? Insects are flying around in here, too."

"My hands are slippery."

To the nurse:

"How did I meet you? by the big door?"

"When was I wrapped up in blankets?"

(Aside to me in a whisper, "What's that nurse's name?")

"'TERRY' Don't jump up, but I want to tell you something when you get a chance."

"Maggie is in that bed next to me reading a magazine!"

"Some other woman is in mother's bed."

"Who's on the floor?"

"You're floating horizontally! You could do one-handed push-ups since you have a disoriented perspective." (He thinks I am the disoriented one??? Ha!)

"Are we going upstairs?"

"Well, GO OUT AND CHECK! You need a hearing aid!"

"Look over the edge of this bed; I've spent a lot of time today throwing things over the side."

"Bring me in some ear plugs because this is a noisy neighborhood."

"Look on the floor for that ball and rag I threw down there."

Many other frantic words and pleas were uttered that day. I knew that he would be losing some physical capacity, but I didn't know he would lose his mind, too. Later, as I staggered out of the hospital into the pouring rain known as Hurricane Floyd, my tears and heartache bowed me low. *Hold us close to you, please, O God*, I whispered. *I'm not sure we're going to make it.*

Thursday, September 16, 1999

We are experiencing the full force of Hurricane Floyd. The route I travel to the hospital is flooded, so I must stay home. I called and talked with Karen, who was able to get there okay. The psychiatrist had visited and with amazing speed decided that Roland is manic-depressive and is in the depressive state due to GBS, thus causing him to be psychotic and hallucinogenic. Will treat these symptoms with two different drugs.

The more I thought about this quick diagnosis, the more puzzled I became. He has never shown any signs whatsoever of being manic-depressive. For the doctor to make such an assessment so casually without any medical history from the patient or me and very little previous medical information to go on is careless and decidedly irresponsible, in my opinion! [Roland later could recall some of the hallucinations that incorporated someone in the room. In this case, he remembered seeing the doctor drive up, park on the edge of a drive, and come to where he was perched precariously on a narrow, upper level seat with a crowd below.]

One of Roland's former students visited, and Roland didn't know who he was but then reacted to him, spoke his name, and told him to watch out for that man behind him. Now we're beginning to wonder if Roland has Lyme Disease that has progressed to a stage of dementia. His condition is poor, and he frantically babbles on and on.

I pace the floor at home crying and feeling despair and total helplessness. Chad spent the entire day baling water from the construction hole just outside our missing basement walls as the rain poured and poured. Two sides of the basement walls had been removed to replace footers and cinder blocks. The plastic sheeting that had been put up had been sufficient protection until Floyd rolled in. *Thank you, God, for Chad being here; for Karen being with Roland today; and, for all our friends and family, who are praying unceasingly for us all. Surely tomorrow will be a better day!*

Friday, September 17, 1999

Roland's decline continues while we and the doctors and nurses discuss whether or not to do a more sophisticated Lyme test; whether or not he is manic-depressive (can one suddenly become manic-depressive??); and whether or not he needs a CAT scan or MRI. Another psychiatrist visited and strongly refuted the previous diagnosis of manic-depression. We do know that sleep deprivation and an ICU syndrome can contribute to hallucinations. Sleep deprivation seems to me to make the most sense as the cause of these frightening hallucinations. I appreciate all the doctors and nurses who are conscientiously and professionally trying as best they can to figure out what is going on so they can treat it.

Although his speech is slurred, he continues to rant and rave at all of us in a pitiful, desperate voice. Here are some of his ramblings as I sat quietly observing him and writing as much down as I could catch. He didn't seem aware of my presence. When he did look at me, it was as though he was looking through me and talking to someone else behind me. We joked that it seems like he doesn't know who we are and that he has a whole new group of friends.

"Chad, take me to the bathroom!"

"Pull the wheelbarrow up!"

"I hear you've had the mumps". (to me; he had seen me across the room crying)

"Jerry Bogard is behind you talking to someone."

"Quick! Get the nurse! He fell down behind the waste basket!"

"I'm standing on a glass washing dishes!"

"Chad is a lawyer, because he turns around things I say."

"Lower the table!"

"Just Dennis do it—not the rest of you!"

"Hurry up, Chad, let's go!"

"How do you do that?"

"Stop it! It's okay, I won't fall!"

"Is Grandma here? How are you doing, Grandma?"

"I didn't chew on it anywhere!"

"Aw shoot!"

Called out for Sherry.

"Move, Bob!" (visitor who walked in). "You're in danger! Get out, get out, get out! [Roland recalls that he imagined he was about to negotiate his release from a tough hostage situation. Bob's approach to the bed to say" How are you, Roland?" was viewed as Bob approaching the van Roland was in and potentially jinxing the whole deal! He recalls that these hallucinations seemed very real and to make perfect sense at the time.]

Toward the end of the day he seemed to know who his visitors were and could come up with their names.

As they rolled Roland out for his MRI, he babbled frantically and seemed so shrunken and frail under the sheet. The puffy hat they put over his hair made him look so woebegone and helpless. He's in another world out of my reach. [Roland recalls the MRI as part of a screening prior to participating in a sting operation! His imaginary life is certainly more exciting that his real life it seems!]

I walked over to the window and looked out on the descending nightfall. From the sixth floor, I could look across the hospital grounds to stores across the way. In the large parking lot people were going about their "important" business—driving, shopping, eating, and getting in and out of their cars with ease. Do they know how lucky they are? Do they appreciate how fabulous and wondrous their bodies and minds are to allow such freedom? How we take even the simplest, most habitual things in our lives for granted. *Oh God, forgive!*

At 10:00 p.m. the infectious disease specialist came in to report that all the tests showed no evidence of Lyme disease present in Roland.

Chad had gone home earlier in the evening in despair and discouragement. Karen and I left Roland, wide-eyed and babbling to his imaginary friends, at midnight and walked, exhausted, through our tears to our cars. *Oh God—we're slipping out of Your hands!*

When the ringing phone awoke me out of a restless sleep at 3:00 a.m., I was frightened to answer it. I knew it was the death call. The resident on duty in ICU was calling to tell me they inserted a breathing tube into Roland because he had too much saliva. I had been asking for a while if perhaps a breathing tube might help Roland, so I was relieved they finally agreed with me.

This was undoubtedly our worst day thus far. GBS, how wicked you are! Can we survive your assault?

Saturday, September 18, 1999

Now that the ventilator is breathing for Roland, he is sleeping peacefully. When occasionally he wakes up, Karen tells him, "It's okay; we're breathing for you now," and he happily goes back to sleep. The nurses, doctors, and we agree that the psychosis was brought on by the devastation of GBS, and this was his only way to handle it.

I ask how long this could go on and am told maybe weeks, maybe months. I'm reassured but filled with uncertainty and panic at the same time. The toll GBS takes on its victims is different for all—with few certainties and widely variable timelines. One thing is certain: it takes a serious toll on loved ones as well as the patient.

We have had so many caring visitors and calls of support. Friends and family all over the country are praying for us.

I don't believe God selected us to endure this hardship for any particular reason, i.e., "to teach Roland patience," as one friend suggested. Instead, I believe this happening is a part of life's trials and tribulations that visit all of us at one time or another. I do believe God is here in our midst giving us good care, support, and love through all of the medical personnel and our many family members and friends. Even though we who are here by Roland's side every day grow weary, we are constantly refreshed by the concern and support of many, many of God's servants (I like to call them angels) holding us up and helping us get through yet another day. And, I am confident God is loving Roland, me, and our family through this crisis. [Roland expressed it this way: stuff happens: how we deal with it is the important part. Feeling the love of God and His caring through the community of all the people who help us makes dealing with hardship much easier.]

Roland peacefully sleeps on. *Thank you, God!* My sister Sue is flying here from Arkansas to help me out on November 6. Thank you, thank you, thank you!

Sunday, September 19, 1999

Roland is still peacefully sleeping but wakes up when the nurses need to check his functions or move him. Then he goes back to sleep. We are told he can sleep for a day or so, but then they will need to increase his activity to keep his lungs clear. The doctor noticed some upper arm and leg movement, which is encouraging. While we talked, Roland wiggled toes on both feet. When I squeezed his toes three times (our "I love you" signal), he flexed his toes back in response. He is with us again. Praise God! He responded to comments to flex upper arms, wiggle toes, stick out his tongue, and open his eyes. Progress! Are we at last on the road up out of this hell?

He was able to nod acknowledgment to visitors. He became agitated one time, and it took me a while to realize I was blocking the fan's breeze on him. We are freezing in here, but he is HOT! The sensation is a common trait of GBS though variable in degree among patients. There is no fever, just a feeling of being hot.

Dennis and his dad put another lock on our downstairs door at home while the house is exposed due to foundation repair. Another example of being cared for. Thank you, Dennis and Joe.

Roland's fingers are swollen, and his wedding band is constricting his finger. Staff will cut the ring off today.

We noticed today an odd smell from Roland—not body odor or dirty smell—just unique. The nurse said this odor is common in GBS patients. They can almost diagnose a GBS patient by that odor alone. Interesting!

About 3:00 a.m. this night/next morning, I awoke and saw something big and round in our bedroom doorway. Frightened, I quickly turned on the light to see that it was a large smiley face balloon—grinning at me—that I had brought home from the hospital. It had drifted down the hall and into our doorway from the living room where I had left it! Gave me something to laugh about. I haven't really laughed in quite awhile, and oh, how I miss laughter!

Monday, September 20, 1999

Roland had a peaceful night. The nurse changed his breathing tube this morning, but he has a fever again today. He nods and tries to communicate with his expressive eyes. It's so frustrating, though, when I just cannot grasp his intent. I think I've finally learned not to stand between the fan and him. Three "I love you" squeezes to his toes give me back three little "I love you" toe flexes. He slept much of today.

Chad is flying back to San Francisco tomorrow to quit his job, load his belongings into his little truck, and drive back here to live with us a while. I'm so thankful for this sacrifice on his part. I didn't ask him to do this; it was his decision. Roland and I have never wanted to be a burden to our children. I hope Chad will not regret this decision someday.

This afternoon the nurses got my rag-doll husband up and into a wheelchair for a little while. He's wearing sneakers for ankle support and is trying to work his hands. He has pneumonia in his right lung and is on antibiotics. The second psychiatrist took him off the manic-depressive medicine and definitely ruled out that condition.

Tonight a handsome young man came to visit us. He has fully recovered from having GBS up to his waist three years ago. His hospital and rehabilitation stay was five to six months. Roland could only nod his thanks to him for coming by. He gave us his phone number and encouraged us to call him at any time. We appreciated his encouragement and hope we can do the same for others someday.

Tuesday, September 21, 1999

Roland nodded to us this morning that he had a bad night last night. Chad came in before catching the shuttle to the airport. We exercised Roland's arms and legs a little to maintain mobility of his joints but were careful not to tire him. He seems to love having his hands, feet, and ankles massaged. Nurses encouraged us to keep encouraging him. *God, please hold us all up; we're flagging!* A new bed with a special air mattress, which should help him be more comfortable, arrived. I left at 4:30 p.m. to go to Karen's to play with granddaughter Emily. A great, fun break for me. Tonight Roland got across to Karen that he wanted to watch TV and enjoyed The Simpsons! Karen says the written "20 Questions" chart helps their communication. So glad he can at least nod his head.

Sherry calls almost every night. I know she is feeling pain at living in Wisconsin and not being close and here more often. She, Tom, and Jesse have been in the process of selling their house and moving into another. I know how she feels. I went through this same situation with my family living in Arkansas. Separation is hard and is especially painful when loved ones are suffering and you're not there physically to share the bad time. We know your love and prayers are with us, Sherry.

Wednesday, September 22, 1999

Roland indicated he slept better last night on the new bed. A larger, nasal feeding tube has been put in, and a tracheostomy is now scheduled for tomorrow or Friday. Also a peg will be inserted in his abdomen for more direct access to his stomach for the feeding tube. An X-ray of sinuses and an ultrasound of legs were done to try to find the source of the continuing fever.

The suctioning of his breathing tube many times a day is hard on him. We can see him cringe when someone comes in the room and announces, "Hi, Mr. Roth, I'm (so-and-so) from respiratory here to suction you!"

The other painful activity for Roland is the almost daily chest x-ray. The technicians first raise the head of the bed to vertical. Roland can't bend his knees so the position stretches his very tight hamstring muscles painfully. Only then do the techs roll in and set up the equipment. He grimaces but can't tell them what is the problem, and they don't notice the pain written on his face. Only later, when he could talk, did I learn of this past stress.

Tonight I left about 6:45 p.m. to go to dinner with a friend. Karen came in to be with her dad. She was able to prop his knees up with a rubber mat (actually a rubber-type of shelf-liner) under his feet to keep his legs from sliding down. (In the earlier days, Roland and the kids devised the mat idea plus a belt around his knees to hold them together!). She thought she saw a hint of a smile at the corner of his mouth. She exercised him some. He is so gaunt and shriveled.

Karen figured out that when he wants an item in the room added to our list of objects and questions, he will look at the item and then quickly roll his eyes over the to the list on the table. I think we're slowly getting better at non-verbal communication. Karen left the hospital at 8:45 p.m.

Thank you, God, for blessing us with these three wonderful children, our two fabulous sons-in-law, and our two precious granddaughters. My heart overflows with love for them.

Thursday, September 23, 1999

I stayed home this morning for a "happy break" with Emily. We went out for a nice walk. The foundation repair is progressing on our basement walls. They used the jackhammer all morning! Dennis picked Emily up at noon, and I got to the hospital by 12:45 p.m. to find Roland sleeping peacefully. The physical therapist came in at 1:20 p.m. and woke him up for a few exercises. Roland was put over into a chair and stayed there about 15 minutes. His lungs sound better today, but he will remain on antibiotics a while longer.

We're still having trouble communicating, and I can see how it really frustrates him. Me, too! A few visitors today. I went to dinner with two friends while Karen was here. Left hospital at 8:10 p.m. My guilt at leaving Roland is becoming a little less as he improves, but he is never out of my mind.

Friday, September 24, 1999

I went to the mall before going to the hospital to buy myself a pair of comfortable shoes to cushion my feet against the hard hospital floors. Arrived at hospital at 11:00 a.m. Roland looks good today and is in good spirits. He slept well last night.

The surgery to replace the breathing and feeding tubes began around 2:00 p.m. I held his hand while they were setting all the equipment up in his room. I held the fan close to him and under his gown to keep him cool. Then I escaped to the waiting room while the procedures were done. The surgery was completed by 3:45 p.m., and he's sleeping now. He looks so much better with those tubes out of his mouth. The trach is inserted into the little dip in his neck just above his sternum. The feeding tube peg is inserted into his stomach. He slept peacefully until 7:00 p.m. Some visitors came in, and he slowly tried to spell out words with his lips for us to lip read. He asked how my mumps were. He still thinks I have had the mumps. He indicated he remembers his psychosis and was anxious about being tied down. Of course, he was not tied down. We understand that later a valve can be put into the trach hole to help him talk.

Karen thinks we've turned the corner now. His smiles and good spirits reassure us that we all will get through this. The patient is now ministering to us!

A friend bought me dinner and another did some grocery shopping for me. *Thank you, God, for so many hands and hearts holding me, and all of us, up to fight this battle.* Chad called from a Pizza Hut in New Mexico on his way home. Safe journey, son.

Saturday, September 25, 1999

I arrived at the hospital about 10:15 a.m. after catching up on a few things around the house. Roland is sleeping peacefully. Some bleeding is occurring around the trach tube, which we understand is normal. He awoke around 11:00 a.m., and I put his sneakers on and positioned his knees up with feet on the bed. We're having trouble again getting him to be comfortable for very long.

The nurse told me, "If several efforts fail, just walk away." I don't think I can give up trying to make him comfortable even though it is frustrating and futile.

The vision in his left eye is fuzzy. Karen came in and gave him a good workout. A friend brought a white erasable board for us to write letters and words on to help communication.

The doctor's check-up today indicated Roland is probably at the plateau stage of this devastating illness. We're as low as we can go; up is the only way we can go now!

Sunday, September 26, 1999

Roland woke up about 6:00 a.m. after a good night's sleep. When I arrived, I put his sneakers on him and exercised his legs. The constant repositioning goes on. He senses some of the nurses' frustration with him, and he is sorry to be so much trouble. Part of the indignity of his condition now is that they put no diaper of any kind on him. He does have a bladder catheter, but his bowel movements pass out onto the bed pad, which bothers him because it's abnormal and an extra burden on the nurses.

To have no control over one's body is, indeed, a horrible thing. We never give this a thought; do we? Oh, how much we do take for granted! This is apparent to me now, over and over. *God. forgive us all.*

Monday, September 27, 1999

Chad rolled in from California this morning at 1:15. Thanks be to God! It's so good to have him home and to have someone else in the house. I did a few errands before arriving at the hospital at 10:15 a.m.

The doctor and the physical therapist are beginning to talk of moving Roland out of ICU and to a "step-down" room for a short while. Also, we need to begin considering rehab hospital options. There's a good one in Newark, New Jersey (where Christopher Reeves was); one near Philadelphia; and one in Wilmington. He cannot go to Wilmington while he is still on the trach. Of course, we want him near home. He may even have to go to a convalescent facility before going to a rehabilitation hospital. Surely hope not.

I feel utterly helpless in trying to decide what we should do. I have no experience with this kind of thing. I'm listening to the advice of the medical professionals and trust that they and God will continue their care and healing in their recommendations.

Tuesday, September 28, 1999

Roland got a new bed last night and had a good night's rest. The respiratory nurses are suctioning out his trach several times a day. A nurse will ask for a speech evaluation to check on swallowing ability and any "gadgets" they might have to assist Roland to speak. Later, they did provide a special "tool" to place on his larynx to magnify his speech efforts. Now we can understand him. He sounds like ET. A while later, he asked me to close his door as I left the room. Later, his trach tube popped out and the buzzer went off, but with the door shut no one could hear it. Until someone did hear it, he breathed on his own.

He's reporting to the nurse that he is beginning again to feel crowded and panicky before going to sleep. So now he's on another medication to calm him. A good bath and shave made him feel much better.

Wednesday, September 29, 1999

This was another day of suctioning, physical therapy, and visitors. Roland yawned for the first time. This small victory reminds me again how we take so much of our amazing bodily functions for granted. To be able to yawn, to scratch where we itch, and to be free to move our bodies around: ALL (and so much more!) are so precious. We just don't realize it until we can't do it. From now on, I promise to feel more grateful and more aware of great, yet seemingly very ordinary, gifts I have been given.

Dennis and Chad had fun raising and lowering the new bed, giving Roland some roller coaster thrills!

Thursday, September 30, 1999

"This is a day of new beginnings", to quote the title of one of Roland's favorite hymns. The ventilator came off, and a valve was placed in the "hole" so Roland can speak. His voice is weak but understandable. *Thank you, thank you, thank you, God!* He said he wants mashed potatoes and applesauce to eat.

Roland was moved to a two-person, step-down room. However, it became needed for two people so he was moved to a one-person room. It is really crowded with all the equipment he still needs. But it's not ICU.

Friday, October 1, 1999

The nurses got Roland up into a "chair-bed" for a short while. He still cannot move on his own so it takes a crew to move him and position him. The few muscles that are active in his trunk tire quickly and begin to spasm so he needs to get back into bed. The nurses must be exhausted, too!

We have decided to go to the Wilmington Hospital rehab unit. We're told the move will likely happen next week. We think family and friend support that has been so valuable will be easier at this close-to-home location as opposed to rehab in a more remote city.

He had a swallowing test this afternoon. They wanted to see if he can swallow water. I went out to an Italian dinner with a group of friends. It was fun and good for me, I suppose. Nevertheless, I missed Roland being there terribly and had that shadow of guilt over me as I do every time I try to do anything for fun or relaxation. I tell myself that I shouldn't feel this way: go ahead; have a good time! But I just can't do it without at least a touch of guilt.

Saturday, October 2, 1999

Roland and I are missing the wedding of Chad's best childhood pal, Tim. Tim's mother, Marlene, one of my best friends, has been diagnosed with pancreatic cancer. So I know this day will be a very, very special and happy day for their whole family. We'll be thinking of them and are so sorry to miss this happy occasion.

Roland was able to swallow a bit of applesauce. Do we ever stop to think what a marvelous gift it is to be able to swallow? *Thank you, God.*

Roland sat in a chair for a while until a small wrinkle in a pad caused his back to hurt. The afternoon filled up with sunshine when our little Emily came into visit Pop Pop. *Thank you, God, for grandchildren.*

Dennis gave Roland a much needed and welcomed shave. A visit on the phone with our Wisconsin children completed a wonderful day.

Sunday, October 3, 1999

Karen shopped for some sweats for Roland to take when he goes to the rehab hospital. Chad came in with a happy report on the wedding. He seated Marlene—what a special duty. Brought tears to my eyes as I remember our 20 years as neighbors, the fun we had, and now the rough patches. I'm confident God is with them as He is with us. He brought us thus far. He won't drop us now, I know.

This afternoon we had visitors who stayed too long, tiring both Roland and me out. Short visits are so much more pleasant and not so exhausting to the patient.

Chad and I thank God and Pizza Hut for sausage pizza. So comforting tonight.

Monday, October 4, 1999

A rainy day today. We're not sure if Roland will move to Wilmington Hospital rehab today as planned. I went to a nearby store and bought Roland a bathrobe and a small suitcase for his big move. Roland had some PT today, which left him pale and tired. The doctor wrote out his release to rehab, which will happen tomorrow. Today was Roland's first day to use the bedpan. Yea! It's amusing to think we're so excited over a bedpan.

As I left the hospital, we were notified Roland will be picked up tomorrow at 9:00 a.m. to move to Wilmington to begin rehab. He will be on the sixth floor, Room 610-B.

Tuesday, October 5, 1999

Chad and I arrived at the hospital by 8:30 a.m. in anticipation of the 9:00 move. We packed up his personal belongings and gathered up all the cards, drawings, gifts, and flowers with which so many people have generously blessed us during this time.

The strong ambulance men arrived promptly at 9:00 a.m. to load Roland onto a stretcher bed to carry him to the waiting ambulance. There is a wonderful shuttle service between here and Wilmington Hospital, which Chad and I used to meet Roland there. I will be able to drive the 15 minutes from our house to here, park, and ride the shuttle directly into Wilmington Hospital, thus avoiding I-95 and parking difficulties. What a blessing for me, a "nervous-Nellie" driver.

When Chad and I arrived at Rehab, Floor 6, we found Roland in Room 612 looking frail, gray, and alone. He lay there limp, wasted, and wide-eyed as though trying to regain strength and hope for this new adventure, whatever it might be. We met the rehab doctor. Then a nurse and a therapist went over all the orientation information. When asked how long she estimated our stay here might be, the therapist said probably no more than three weeks.

Roland is having some severe skin itching that started last night. He was able to suck on some ice chips and ate a container of custard.

The nurse call button is pinned on the pillow by his head so he can just roll his head onto it to call for help. Hope it works!

Wednesday, October 6, 1999

The amazing event today was watching four nurses arrange a strong, sling-type apparatus under Roland, which then was hooked onto a "crane" to slowly lift him from the bed, swing him around, and lower him into a wheelchair. We were all breathless after this precarious operation.

Therapy takes place regularly every day. Saturday and Sunday have only abbreviated morning sessions. Respiratory is still providing some treatment even though the pneumonia is gone. The therapy sessions take place in other very spacious, well-equipped rooms. The full morning regimen—breakfast, wash up, bedpan time, and being dressed by 9 a.m. followed by occupational, speech, and recreational therapy —leaves him exhausted by noon. His rear hurts so badly from sitting in the chair for 3 hours that he wants to get back into bed, but with lunch approaching and physical therapy (PT) shortly thereafter, he must stay in the chair. After PT, naptime is a welcomed event.

Roland tried eating his lunch and dinner in the dining room with other rehab patients. Breakfast is in bed each day. However, he feels awkward and self-conscious having to be fed by an aide among other patients who are able to feed themselves—and he wants to be in his bed. He will eat lunch and dinner in his room from now on.

Thursday, October 7, 1999

More pureed food went down well today. Now that Roland is eating again, friends are volunteering happily and willingly to visit at meal time just to feed Roland. Karen made up a schedule of volunteers so we know who will be coming to feed Roland for every meal. It is a tender and blessed sight to watch friends feed Roland. I see Jesus in all these people—tenderly and patiently feeding a helpless friend.

Since Week 1, Karen has been conducting Roland's freshman seminar weekly, along with her other work duties. Thank you, Karen, for taking all these additional tasks upon your busy self! We are so fortunate.

Roland sat in the chair in PT for one hour, which tired him. The staff psychologist did an extensive interview today to check for depression and anxiety. Roland's weight today is 154 pounds, down 23 pounds from his hospital admission weight a month ago.

Friday, October 8, 1999

Today was a scary day in PT. The therapist lifted Roland out onto a "tilt board", which he slowly tilted into a vertical position. It was a milestone. However, it was a bit panicky, too, since only the straps and therapists' hands—nothing Roland could do—could keep him upright. It made him feel weak and dizzy because his muscle tone is still too weak to sustain his blood pressure in that position.

Roland's eyes are red, burning, and filled with mucous. The staff opthamologist will come in to check them. Add one more doctor to the long, long list of different doctor specialists we've met on this road.

Saturday, October 9, 1999

Weekends seem long here. All therapy is abbreviated, and it feels to Roland as though these days are wasted and slowing his progress. My view is that he's working his body hard and needs these days to rest. He became woozy again in OT today, cutting the session short. He seems sad and dejected today. Thus far, his good spirits and positive outlook have been amazing and an inspiration to all of us.

Chad shaved Roland, and I flossed Roland's teeth. He has a fever of 101, probably from the eye infection. The valve in his trachea honks occasionally and has to be cleaned out. A low day today. After a few times, the honking becomes a very irritating sound. We mustn't let the blues get a hold on us! Have I prayed lately? Sometimes I feel like I'm just stumbling through these days, weary and in a fog.

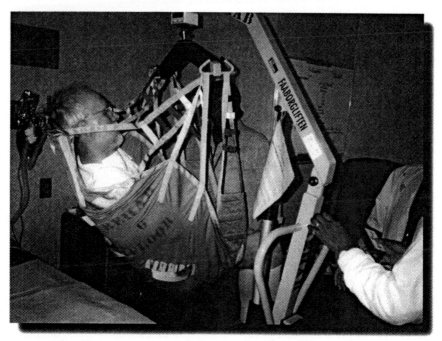

Getting from wheelchair to bed in lift

Sunday, October 10, 1999

Roland's spirits have perked up. Occupational therapy worked on his hands and arms today. We are sorry to miss Sunday chapel services since they take place when his therapy is scheduled.

Roland now has a urinary infection. The honking of the valve is really getting on all our nerves.

Chad took Roland on a wheelchair outing—a cruise up and down the halls of Floor 6. Roland looks longingly out the window at the beautiful trees turning to flame in the cemetery across the street. How he must quietly be yearning to feel and smell the autumn days moving into their full glory now!

Monday, October 11, 1999

A close friend brought us some delicious soup and muffins. Truly a comfort food blessing. The leg exercises in PT were rigorous. Again, Roland got dizzy when the therapist tried to get him vertical. Face exercises are now part of the therapy program. I suppose this is to work on the one eye and side of the mouth that still droop a bit.

Tuesday, October 12, 1999

This morning I took Roland's glasses to his optician for adjustment. When I arrived at the hospital, Roland was just returning to his room from speech therapy. In recreation therapy (which he does not like), he practiced dropping blocks into a bucket. He joked how he can keep up with his one-year-old granddaughters now.

A husband and wife stopped in to encourage us. The man had been stricken in July with GBS and spent August in this very bed rehabilitating. He is using only one crutch now and has just been given the okay to drive again. Visits by survivors of GBS spread so much hope and encouragement. We agree we hope we can do the same someday.

Another new doctor stopped in to say a new antibiotic would be tried in an against the urinary infection, which may have been caused by the catheter.

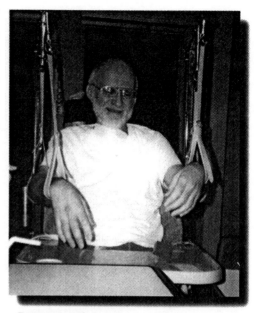

Recreational therapy: picking up blocks with arms in slings

Wednesday, October 13, 1999

Not much new today. However, Roland was able to enjoy "regular" food—macaroni and cheese and green beans. In PT he was able to sit up by himself without support for a few minutes. He said, "I feel like a newborn calf!"

I went home early with a headache, which I rarely have. I worked in the yard a while and rested. Every day I push to the back of my mind the question, *What is going to be the eventual outcome of this?* and *How long, O God, how long will this last?* No answers come out of the blue, so we plod on—step by step—trusting God will be with us.

Thursday, October 14, 1999

Roland got a shampoo and hair cut—the first, I think, since GBS took over his life. He felt and looked so much better afterward. Karen came in tonight. She cut and filed his nails, brushed his teeth, exercised his limbs and face, and read his cards to him. How thankful I am to have Karen and Dennis (and Emily) and Chad nearby. They come in with cheer and new vigor when I'm worn out. I long for Sherry, too, and know she supports us long distance and cheers us with calls and new reports of Jesse's daily changes and adventures. We are deeply blessed.

Friday, October 15, 1999

Today is a gorgeous fall day. On the way to and from the hospital on the shuttle, I enjoy the trees along the highway as they begin their fall color show. This is a valuable time when I can just sit back, feel my body relax a bit, and soak up the beautiful autumn colors. Some people say that fall is a dying time. I see only its beauty. To me the grand glory before the trees become bare is a promise that beauty and life will return. I try to apply my belief to this illness as well. We are in a barren, cold time now. Beauty and a new life will surely follow someday. Roland was able to sit alone for about 30 minutes today. He took a long nap this afternoon.

Saturday, October 16, 1999

Chad is writing in the diary today. Regina stayed home to go to a funeral, bake an apple cake, and have an early birthday dinner for Karen. Here's what he recorded:

"Nurse Ratchett" is on duty. She told Dad he needed to be going to the bathroom (bowel movements) at night instead of complicating the morning procedures. She gruffly told him he needed to sit in the chair more, even if he was uncomfortable doing so. Her 28 years of nursing give her definite expertise!

Only one hour of PT today.

Sunday, October 17, 1999

It is a rainy day. Our spirits start out sort of drab, too. "Nurse Ratchett" is on duty again today. Up until this nurse, all of the nurses and staff we've been in contact with have been kind and so patient. I think "Nurse Ratchett" has the ability to be so, too. The nurses are overworked and must attend to so many, many details. They do a magnificent job, and we are totally grateful for their excellence. I think "Nurse Ratchett" is weary. We don't know what troubles she may be carrying. We'll try to help her. (Roland later confides that his goal is to get her to smile before he leaves.)

Physical therapy was one hour again today. Roland worked really hard at sitting up on his own. He sat in his chair as I fed him lunch and we looked out at the glorious trees. Various friends brought in a basket of gourds, today's church bulletin, and some soothing body lotion. One of Roland's brothers called, and Roland talked while I held the phone to his ear.

Tonight several nurses and aides will try to roll Roland in a special shower chair into the shower. He still has some of the GBS smell about him.

I wrote thank-you notes, but I don't think I can ever fully convey how much thanksgiving we feel for all that so many dear people have done for us. The simplest things seem to be the most powerful—prayer, a basket of gourds, a fork raised to hungry lips of one whose hands are useless. Tears of thanksgiving are flowing now.

Monday, October 18, 1999

Another beautiful fall day with a nice gentle breeze. After PT late in the afternoon, I pushed Roland outside in the wheelchair. Except for the brief transfer to this hospital, this is the first time he has felt fresh air since September 3rd. There is a nice park-like area near the hospital where I can sit by him, and we can enjoy the fall day together. I know he marvels at people briskly walking by and knows they probably do not realize how fortunate they are. It was hard going back into the hospital. I wanted to run off with him and leave this nightmare behind. Oh well, not yet.

Chad came in and fed Roland yummy meatloaf, accompanied, of course, by applesauce, a taste and practice of Roland's since childhood and one not to be denied in the hospital, even if he had to teach his feeders to dip the meat into the applesauce before feeding it to him!

Tuesday, October 19, 1999

I arrived after recreation therapy just as nurses were getting Roland back into bed and onto the bedpan. He has managed to convince them that he really needs to get back in bed during lunch break. The bedpan activity usually lasts about 30 minutes. Even with the curtain drawn around him, I sense his frustration and lack of privacy as people are in and out of the room talking and assisting his roommate. Just one more indignity to overcome.

In PT, Roland tolerated 90° on the tilt table without getting dizzy. He lasted three to four minutes before his back and knees grew tired. Now, he can somewhat control his right leg when it's flexed up.

Went home on the shuttle at 6:00 p.m. Karen came in this evening. We leave notes for each other as we pass like ships in the dark.

Wednesday, October 20, 1999

I babysat and had fun with Emily this morning. Arrived at the hospital about 2:00 p.m., as Roland was finishing up therapy. His therapist encourages us by saying Roland seems to be getting stronger. Roland sneezed today for the first time! Nerves and muscles are slowly, so slowly, waking up. Roland's dental hygienist, daughter of a church friend, came in today and graciously gave him a good dental cleaning. So appreciative of her doing that. He now weighs 151.

Thursday, October 21, 1999

Today in PT Roland leaned forward as if to stand from a sitting position on the side of the low therapy table. It is very scary for him, like leaning out over a cliff, he says. His legs are not ready yet. Still, the therapist notes progress. The rest of the day included a long nap, facial exercises, and guests. Some of the members of his student Wildlife Conservation Club brought a nice collage they had made. Almost daily, we wonder about Roland's professorship job at the University of Delaware. Will he be able to keep his job? Will the paychecks keep coming? We have excellent insurance through the University, for which we are most grateful, but will it run out? I'm afraid to ask anyone, though I know I should. I'm just burying my head in the sand, I guess! A new roommate today.

Friday, October 22, 1999

Happy 33rd birthday to Karen today! She and Dennis are off for a well-deserved vacation they had planned before Roland became ill. They're going to the Grand Canyon and Las Vegas. Dennis' parents will be here with Emily this weekend, and I'll get to play with her until her parents return Thursday.

When I arrived at the hospital, Roland was in recreation therapy sadly trying to paint a birdhouse with his arms supported in slings on the chair. I choked up watching him struggle to do something so simple. I could see the hurt and frustration in his face; his hands were misshapen and struggling awkwardly to grasp the paintbrush; his body was shriveled and stooped, useless. It reminded me of watching a child trying in vain to accomplish a task much too advanced for the child.

Later, after PT, we journeyed out into the fresh air and the hopefulness that the day's beauty would bring back to our hurt spirits. I have a flash of that children's book about the little engine that could —"I think I can, I think I can, I think I can . . ."

Saturday, October 23, 1999

Chad is spending today with Roland while I take a day off for a hair appointment and yard work. The boys enjoyed watching football together. Chad got the distinct privilege of cleaning out Roland's nose, another example of a personal hygiene task that Roland must rely on others to do for him. Roland slept some and kept jumping awake calling out crazy comments. Surely hope the hallucinations aren't returning!

Sunday, October 24, 1999

I arrived at the hospital by 10:00 a.m. and helped Roland get dressed. I only partly enjoyed my day off yesterday because my mind was here with him, and I missed him.

One hour of PT today. Guests visited in the afternoon of this beautiful day. Roland has a new "Texas Catheter," which keeps popping off—not a good thing.

Monday, October 25, 1999

I'm home again all day today with Emily. She keeps me happily distracted. Chad was able to get to the hospital by 4:15 p.m. Roland reported he did well on the tilt table and completed two sides of that dumb birdhouse. Another catheter popped today. Something must be done. A funny aide later said, "Get me some duct tape; I'll make it stay on."

Another new roommate today. Roland was able to select his meals from the regular menu that most of the other patients use.

Tuesday, October 26, 1999

I dropped Emily off at her daycare at 8:00 a.m. and headed to the hospital. When I arrived, Roland was in another room having an EMG test. This is an uncomfortable test with needle pricks and mild electric pulses to get an idea how much nerve damage has occurred.

I straightened up Roland's side of the room. It was a wreck. Later, we had a conference with the doctor regarding the EMG results. The doctor reported that extensive axon damage had occurred. The axon is the core of a nerve. Therefore, the doctor said recovery from this deep nerve damage will be long as re-growth of the axon is very slow. I asked the doctor to guess whether or not a complete recovery can reasonably be expected. He replied he is "conservatively optimistic." I didn't take that as a hopeful comment.

We will have a family conference with the doctor and all the therapists on November 4 to discuss progress and a possible discharge date. We went outside to our favorite spot. We didn't talk much today as we both poured over a lot of "what ifs" in our minds. Our lives have changed, and I think we're facing more challenging changes. It's hard to let hope and a positive attitude always have the upper hand over fear, dread, and the unknown. *Hang on to us, God! I know You're here with us, but my mind is leaping ahead and not living this day in trust and confidence.*

Wednesday, October 27, 1999

This morning Chad and I drove to the airport to pick up Sherry and Jesse arriving from Madison for a visit. It is *so* good to see them. We went straight to the hospital to share the joy with Roland. Roland had a shower last night; today, a shave, good friends and his family all here. We are so grateful. Roland fell into a wonderful nap lulled by the sounds of a classical music tape, which included bird songs (given to him by one of his students).

Thursday, October 28, 1999

Today was the last of the tube feeding: a can of protein supplement at night, which had been in addition to a can of the supplement at each meal to ensure he got all the proper nutrients. He is eating well enough now that the tube can come out of his stomach. Chad and we girls stayed most of the day. The granddaughters make us all laugh and raise our spirits.

Karen and Dennis returned safely tonight from a wonderful vacation.

Friday, October 29, 1999—Saturday, October 30, 1999

I stayed home this morning and baked another apple cake, Roland's favorite, and did grocery shopping. Karen and Sherry spent time with their dad and fed him lunch. Jesse and I went in later. She helped me feed Pop Pop dinner even though you can tell his appearance scares her a little bit. Roland tried to push Jesse in her stroller from his wheelchair as part of his therapy. It was difficult. Roland weighed 157 pounds today. The gains should help him get over his hollow-eyed, gaunt look.

Sunday, October 31, 1999

Emily visited Pop Pop today in her witch costume. Sherry and Jesse stopped by for a last brief visit before leaving with Chad for the airport. It was a tearful farewell. Parting gives me that awful ache inside. Roland puts on a brave front. This afternoon we enjoyed a warm hour outside soaking up this lovely fall day. This quiet, meditative time helps get our thoughts and moods back into a more positive, hopeful mode.

Monday, November 1, 1999

Another absolutely beautiful 70° day. I had an eye exam and errands to do before getting to the hospital in time to feed Roland lunch. We enjoyed our spot outdoors again after PT.

Chad is home cleaning up our basement and putting everything back in order after the wall reconstruction. It has been a dusty mess, and I couldn't face cleaning it up myself. Thank you, Chad.

Roland's physical therapist came to visit our home tonight to see if Roland can manage living here upon his hospital discharge. For 23 years, we've lived in this split-level house with steps going both up and down from the entranceway. The therapist measured the door openings, halls, and spaces through which Roland's wheelchair would need to pass. When the therapist finished measuring, we sat down for a frank talk.

There is no way we can care for Roland here in this home when he is discharged. We don't know now if he will ever be able to function out of a wheelchair. We really need to move to a one-level house. Roland and I had talked about moving to a ranch-style house someday—when we got old! Well, someday is *now*, I guess.

I spent a long time in bed tonight staring wide-eyed at the ceiling. Sleep wouldn't come. Not even tears. Not even prayers except, *"How, O God, can I do this?"*

Tuesday, November 2, 1999

Karen called a realtor for us to begin looking for any ranch houses that might be for sale now. I watched the occupational therapist form and complete arm and wrist supports for Roland to wear at night. Very interesting. He has also been wearing some big grey fuzzy boots at night to prevent foot drop. I watched Roland in recreation therapy.

Some days he just reads the newspaper, which he most likes to do in there. The therapist puts a long stick into Roland's mouth. The stick has a rubber tip on the other end. With the stick, he can turn the pages by moving his head, but he still needs some help with the task. He still hates recreation therapy; it's the only therapy where he tries to slack off from what he is asked to do. There's nothing fun about recreation when you can't do it!

Wednesday, November 3, 1999

This is a field trip day for some of the patients. They, including Roland, are carefully and slowly loaded onto a bus. The wheelchair lift for Roland's chair was a new experience for him. I was waiting to meet the bus at the Delaware Nature Society's Ashland Nature Center. Roland has been active in DNS, so he has been looking forward to this trip. The patients all shuffled in or were wheeled into the gathering room for a talk and a chance to see and hold various animals. As the speaker placed a frog in Roland's hands, the frog—excuse me —"pooped" into his hand much to everyone's delight!

Roland really enjoyed seeing his friends who work here. It was so good to get away from the hospital for a few hours. I watched in the parking lot as the therapists and aides loaded all the helpless patients back onto the bus. As the bus slowly rolled away and Roland's hopeful smile and limp body disappeared down the road, I stood there and cried, giving in to all-consuming pity for him, for me, for our changed lives. So many emotions tumbling around in me—anger, sorrow, hopelessness, fear. I remind myself that God's arms are around me, and I give over my unhappiness to Him. I remember nothing about the drive home this late fall afternoon.

Thursday, November 4, 1999

Roland had a good day in therapy today. He was able to sit alone on the table mat. Then the therapist used a board with roller beads on it to slide Roland off the mat and into his wheelchair. It was a struggle, but he made it. This morning the surgeon removed the stomach feeding tube. Roland said it was not painful, just a soft pop.

A summary of today's family and staff conference follows: Axon and other nerve damage has occurred, and the extent of possible recovery is unknown. Progress is seen in Roland's weight, ability to eat, and ability to shift his weight to avoid sores. His skin is in good condition with only minor irritations. The down side is that Roland needs to be here at least 30 more days, an electric wheelchair is being ordered, our home is not wheelchair accessible, and major support is still needed for daily personal activities. A representative from a rehabilitation hospital near Philadelphia as present to hear the report. If she thinks that her hospital can be of more service than this one, she will contact us soon. Our feeling is that the services here are excellent, and we really don't want to move. The family and community support we've had here would not be possible there. We think this loving support is a major boost in Roland's outlook and recovery progress. This support is a major factor in helping me cope as well.

Friday, November 5, 1999

I stayed with Roland only two hours this morning. Then I went home and out with a realtor to look at available, appropriate houses for us. We looked at a number of houses, but none excited me too much. I think I'm overwhelmed with the thought of cleaning out our home of 23 years, still a haven for Roland, the "pack rat never-throw-anything-away-you-might-need-it-someday person." How can the kids and I possibly do this? Buying and selling houses plus moving is daunting enough without a paralyzed husband's needs to also consider. *Oh God, I need to ask you, again, for strength, PLEASE!*

Saturday, November 6, 1999

I got a flu shot this morning. A warning on the form I signed indicated a possible side effect might be Guillain-Barré Syndrome. I wonder how many people know what they are signing off! Apparently, the warning is there because a number of people developed GBS in 1976 after receiving the swine flu vaccination.

Today was a ho-hum day at the hospital. We were able to go outside for a little while. Later Roland watched Wisconsin beat Purdue in football. He also thought a "Bobbie" sub (turkey, dressing, and cranberry sauce) sounded good to him.

Sunday, November 7, 1999

My sister, Sue, arrived last night from Arkansas. It is wonderful to have her here for her moral support as well as her hands in holding me together. She is taking time away from her husband, her daughter, and her job to come cheer me up and give me encouragement. I am truly thankful.

Roland's 87-year-old mother in Arkansas has been ill but is now home from the hospital. She calls us frequently but is not able to come out here. Roland's two older brothers and cousins call us also, but none is able to come out. They, as with so many others, hold us close in prayer, and we are grateful.

Sue and I spent the day at the hospital.

Monday, November 8, 1999

This morning Sue, Dennis, Karen, the realtor, and I went to have a second look (for me) at a house near our current home that is for sale. The main floor is wheelchair accessible with only one door that would need to be widened. The master bedroom and bath are on the main floor. There is a long staircase upstairs to two more bedrooms and a bath. Sue and I also went to look at a cottage available in a senior citizen community. It is definitely too small.

Dennis is working at our house repairing the kitchen ceiling where we had taken down a large fluorescent fixture and installed a light and ceiling fan just before Roland got sick. Looking around the house, I notice many things that need to be done before we can put the house on the market. I can't think about that right now. I'm Scarlett O'Hara—I'll think about that tomorrow.

Tuesday, November 9, 1999

I see Roland has been in rehab five weeks now. The 3-week stay predicted on our first day here was a bit optimistic! In PT Roland practiced trying to roll over. So hard. He kind of looks like an overturned turtle struggling to right itself. Roland did stand up a few seconds with a therapist holding him on both sides and blocking his knees. Yea!

Another beautiful day. We take advantage of it and go outside a while. Since our beating from Hurricane Floyd, the weather has been exceptionally glorious this fall. What a wonderful gift!

Wednesday, November 10, 1999

Early this morning, I met with the realtor's financial officer to discuss buying a house before selling the one we have now. He totally overwhelmed me, and I left there with my head spinning and thinking: *How, oh how, are we going to do this?*

Just as I got home, the phone rang. Roland had asked someone to call me and put the phone up to his ear. He, too, had been thinking during the night. He said, "Let's drop this buying another house right now and check out a wheelchair accessible apartment for a while." This would make an extra move for me to do! But maybe it would be worth it in the long run.

So, Sue and I headed off to about the only wheelchair accessible apartments around here. The one available in early December has two bedrooms, two baths, and feels airy and spacious. The windows look out onto nice woods. Even though it will be expensive to pay this rent while we still maintain a house, I decide we'll take it. It feels right. The decision made, I feel an enormous sense of relief.

At the hospital today, Karen watched as the occupational therapist taught Roland how to get in and out of the bathtub by sliding on a board from the wheelchair onto a shower chair. He also tried brushing his teeth with an electric toothbrush. A friend brought in a delicious apple pie. Roland was fitted for the electric wheelchair. Progress! Why do I feel so unsure?

Thursday, November 11, 1999

This morning Sue and I met Roland's OT at the model apartment so she could check out its accessibility, measure doorways, sink and toilet heights, etc. She gave her okay, and I put down our deposit. The apartment will be available for us to move into on December 8.

I'm so thankful to all the people who faithfully show up at the hospital to feed Roland and keep him company. This has allowed me freedom to attend to these other matters. The schedule Karen worked out permits co-workers, students, and other friends from church and elsewhere to sign up for a meal that is convenient for them. We feel so cared for and loved by a vast community of unselfish, caring friends. I cannot ever adequately express my deep, deep thankfulness. The word "community" has a whole new meaning to us now as does the term "church family." How could we have survived thus far without them? They surely are sent by God. He does work in wondrous ways!

Friday, November 12, 1999

This morning Sue and I finalized the apartment rental paperwork. I committed to rent it for three months with another two-months-at-a-time renewal option.

Roland continues to work himself into exhaustion in PT. With the therapist's help, Roland was able to lie on his stomach for a while, the first time since August!

Saturday, November 13, 1999

This morning Chad and I reluctantly drove Sue to the Baltimore airport to catch her flight home. She has given me such a needed boost. I hate to see her leave. When we returned home, I caught up on laundry before picking-up the Bobbie sub for which Roland has been hungering.

Roland and I spent the afternoon alone watching football. We normally don't watch much TV, but here it really helps the long weekend days pass more quickly.

Late this afternoon, we were blessed by a visit from two couples. A university couple brought their good friends from Virginia to see us. The man from Virginia had GBS in 1998 and is now recovered. He has lingering numbness in his fingertips and on the bottom of his feet. Tears came to his eyes when he saw Roland lying there unable to do any more than to say, "Hello, come on in."

We swapped stories for about an hour, and they advised us not to leave rehab too soon. We appreciated their visit very much even though it brought back many sad memories for them.

Sunday, November 14, 1999

Another slow day, but Roland seemed to be in happier spirits after the encouraging visit we had yesterday. Karen spent today here. She groomed Roland and took him outside after the one hour of PT. I relaxed at Karen's and played with Emily.

Roland was able to sit on the edge of the bed a while after being pushed, pulled, tugged, and dragged into this position. He is dead weight, so it really is hard for us to situate him without help.

Monday, November 15, 1999

Good therapy today. Nothing new to report. Chad gave Roland a shave. A few friends stopped by. Chad helped in the transfer of Roland from the bed to the wheelchair. We all need to know how to do these transfers safely. Hope we can remember when we get home!

Tuesday, November 16, 1999

When I arrived in the recreation therapy room this morning, I saw Roland with his back to me, hunched over with a long stick in his mouth, trying desperately to turn the pages of the newspaper. One arm was in some kind of support, uselessly trying to help. Tears stung my eyes as I watched and recalled the vigorous, active, energetic husband I had only two months ago. How quickly we can lose all bodily functions for which we rarely give a grateful thought.

Again and again, I'm brought up short thinking of all the physical blessings (the real miracle, Roland had often insisted) that we thoughtlessly take for granted. *Oh, God, please forgive.*

Wednesday, November 17, 1999

I wheeled Roland downstairs to visit the notary on the premises to assist us in signing the apartment lease. Of course, he is unable to sign anything. During PT, I had to practice over and over the procedure for transferring Roland from the raised mat into his chair. I keep wanting him to help! Then I remember. Am I going to be able to do this when we get home? Am I going to be able to get him in and out of the car? How will I ever get him into bed? (To SLEEP, that is; that question has a new meaning these days! Ha Ha!) *Get ready, God. I think I'm going to need You more than ever before.*

Thursday, November 18, 1999

Roland weighs 158. Chad was able to come in and give Roland another shave, a milkshake, and some good stretching. Karen came in this evening, and good friends were here for their "turn" at feeding Roland dinner.

Some of Roland's students were here today receiving advice about their research. I know Roland is missing teaching and his daily contact with students. I know he's trying NOT to think about how far behind he is in all his assorted work duties. He's doing a good job accepting this awful thing happening to him, and he is just going to focus on getting well no matter how long it takes! Roland *never, ever,* says, "Why me?"

Progress today. While lying flat on his back, Roland could turn his left hand over and back. The right arm and hand are not able to do this yet. Earlier today, sitting at a table, Roland could raise his left forearm three times with his elbow on the table.

Sherry called to check on how we are doing. Jesse is starting to say, "No!" The fun begins. Life goes on.

Friday, November 19, 1999

Today's OT focused on our practicing transferring Roland between the shower chair and wheelchair. I'm so afraid I'll do something wrong, and he'll splat on the floor.

Now the catheter is out, and the nurses bring Roland a urinal to use. We were able to enjoy another gorgeous fall afternoon outdoors.

Saturday, November 20, 1999

Roland only had stretch therapy today. He can hardly wait for Saturday and Sunday to pass so he can get back into the real therapy though the stretching feels very good.

We were able to go outside for a nice, long spell. We're so grateful for this warm fall, which permits us to soak up some lovely moments outside of the hospital's dreary confines. The gift of these glorious days takes some of the sting out of this situation that has befallen us. I'm seeing some beauty in the midst of the ugly. *Thank You, God!*

It was a rocking Saturday night. I had to do some nose clipping and excavating. We watched TV and ate pumpkin pie brought by a friend. I'm just glad he's alive and we are together.

Lonely, late night ride back home on the shuttle. As I stand, alone, outside the hospital in the dark night waiting on the shuttle to arrive, I almost start to slide back into fear, loneliness, and pity. Then, I remember the beautiful day we've had, all the friends and family who are supporting us, all of the medical personnel who work hard to mend Roland, that we are alive, and God still loves us.

The bus arrives, and I step on to head home to rest and once again remember to whisper "thank you" to God.

Sunday, November 21, 1999

The temperature hit 70 degrees today. Chad enjoyed spinning Roland outdoors and around a few blocks. Both Karen and Chad tell me Dad needs his toenails clipped. Shall we draw straws to see who the lucky winner will be?

Monday, November 22, 1999

When I arrived, Roland was in recreation therapy trying to play dominos with that blasted stick in his mouth. He didn't look like he was having much fun.

The happiest moment of his day, I think, is when he can leave this room. Thank goodness we are able to go outside, which seems to "recreate" him more than anything else—with no stick in the mouth either.

Tuesday, November 23, 1999

The therapist coached us on transferring Roland to and from bed and wheelchair. We had lunch out. Well, actually, I pushed him to the downstairs coffee shop I've frequented while here. I fed him a BLT, french fries, and tea. What glory!

We took milkshakes outside even though it was drizzling a bit. We did pretty well on our own (transferring him from wheelchair into bed) when we got back inside. He didn't even mind that I fell over on top of him as I lost my balance as soon as I plopped him down onto the bed! Good laugh!

While flat on his back with his left arm on his chest, Roland was able to slowly move his hand up to his nose to scratch it. I cannot even imagine what it must be like to have an itch somewhere and not be able to scratch it for relief. I also think about how much I flop back and forth in bed at night getting myself comfortable. How awful it must be to have to lie on your back and not be able to move any part of your body at all—all night. I think I would go nuts! Yet Roland never complains or whines about what he can't do. His faith and positive attitude are amazing to all who witness it.

Wednesday, November 24, 1999

I feel hopeful that we will one day soon be free of hospital confinement. With the assistance of Chad, Dennis, and our physical therapist, we were able to transfer Roland successfully from his wheelchair into our truck. I think we can do it on our own.

Tonight, when close friends came to feed Roland, they brought along a large bag, a special treat for later, they announced. Roland can now sit on the side of the bed with his feet propped up as he is fed meals. After dinner, the friends lifted Roland's feet and placed them inside the bag. As Roland moved his feet around inside the bag, he heard a rustling, crunchy sound. Roland's feet were in contact with crisp, fallen leaves of all colors. With our friends' efforts and Roland's simple leg movements, he could sense again that wonderful sound of feet crunching fallen leaves while walking along a path in autumn. What a simple act of joyfulness we appreciate now more than ever. I am filled anew with a fresh wave of thanks to God for this wonderful fall activity we almost forgot about and for loving friends who helped us remember it. Sometimes the simplest things are really the most magnificent! Praise God!

Thursday, November 25, 1999—Thanksgiving Day

Thanksgiving has always been my favorite holiday, this year more than ever before. Chad and Dennis drove to the hospital, loaded Roland into the truck, and brought him to Karen and Dennis' home to join Emily, Chad, Dennis' parents, sister and brother-in-law, and me for the day. Roland's transfer from the truck into his wheelchair involved our pushing, pulling, lifting, sliding, or offering encouragement. For lack of a ramp, Dennis and Chad lifted Roland and his chair up the front steps. No prayer and blessing of praise and thanksgiving before a meal has ever been more heartfelt and sincere! There are

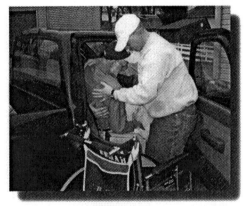

Thanksgiving 1999—Dennis and Chad (in truck) unloading Roland

no words to describe my deep thanksgiving for my husband by my side and all the spiritual and physical caring of so many people this year. Language is inadequate and seems superficial.

Roland enjoyed home cooking, football on TV, and a nice nap before reluctantly being carried back to the hospital around 8:00 this evening. Chad and Dennis drove him by his office and our house on the return trip to the hospital. Thanksgiving Day may just be a holiday on the calendar for some, but Thanksgiving for me, now, is every moment, every day.

Friday, November 26, 1999

This routine day with therapy was brightened by a visit from out-of-town special friends. Later, I groomed Roland's nails for him. A loyal friend fed Roland dinner and brought him homemade cookies.

Saturday, November 27, 1999

Another quiet day around the hospital with only abbreviated therapy and my urgent feeling of needing to do some Christmas shopping.

Sunday, November 28, 1999

With assistance in therapy, Roland stood up and found it to be slightly less strenuous than before. This morning I attended Sunday school and church for the first time since August. So many people asked for updates on Roland and reassured me of their continuing prayers for us.

This afternoon Roland discovered he could change the TV channel with the remote control under his elbow. He was not able to do the changing with the remote on his chest because his fingers are not strong enough to press the buttons. The nurse call button is pinned to the pillow, which allows him to press the button with his head. This usually works. Sometimes, however, it slides out of reach, and he has to lie there helplessly until someone happens to come into the room. This happened during the night several times causing him to do some powerful "self-talk" to stifle rising panic. I get sweaty and greatly agitated just thinking about needing help and not being able to move. I suppose he could call out for help though his vocal muscles are still weak, and his voice is not strong yet. He says that he thinks of people who have survived days of being pinned down in earthquake debris and figures he is better off.

Monday, November 29, 1999

I arrived at the hospital while Roland was in therapy to learn he was to be moved to another room and to the bed away from the window for the "hospital's convenience". This put me in a tizzy, asking *why, why, why?* I "consulted" with the Patient Relations Department and the head nurse as I started to move his belongings and decorations. Roland also was not pleased when he returned from therapy and was taken to the new room. Shortly after lunch, we learned that he could return to his original room.

I'm afraid all the pent-up stress and strain of the last three months came unleashed in my tantrum today. I'm sorry for this, but I am relieved the hospital personnel honored our feelings about the room change, which probably didn't seem all that significant to them. However, the thought of losing that restorative window view and the familiarity he had with that space was disturbing to Roland and to me. If this incident could set me off so easily, I'm wondering how well I'm *really* coping with this illness. How am I going to hold up when we get Roland home to our "new" home, the apartment? *Can I do this, God? Only with Your strength and blessing. I am weak and so tired.*

Tuesday, November 30, 1999

Roland was able to stand up again shakily a few minutes in therapy. This sounds like such a little thing but is a great miracle to us!

Wednesday, December 1, 1999

Roland's therapy practice included trying to stand up part-way to get his pants on. Then we practiced the transfer from the wheelchair onto the toilet. Again, this is a marvelous happening, to us. Do people realize how wonderful it is to dress themselves or to go to the toilet when they want to—unassisted and in private?

Thursday, December 2, 1999

More transfer practice today from wheelchair to toilet. We also practiced pulling his pants down as well as up. No more comment here!

One week from today we go *home!* Apartment home, that is. Will we miss this hospital home? Not a chance!

Friday, December 3, 1999

When I arrived at the hospital, Roland was in recreational therapy playing Parcheesi with the therapist. It was more work than fun, I think, and tired him out. The simplest things he *cannot* do seem to hit him the hardest in this therapy. Sometimes in these therapy sessions he seems almost mad. If he ever really feels anger about what's happened to him, it seems almost to break through in recreation therapy and seems to me to be just below the surface—like he really would like to cry or throw things or yell out in frustration. Seeing this really breaks my heart, and I'm glad when we can flee back to his room.

One of the candidates for taking over Roland's spring classes came by to do a brief interview with Roland.

I will be forever grateful to the University of Delaware for continuing Roland's employment. People from this University and the College of Agriculture and Natural Resources have not only visited but have included Roland in a lot of decision-making and have shared with him the daily events there. So many present and former students have sent cards and flowers or have come personally to cheer him on. One drove here from Ohio in the face of Hurricane Floyd just to visit Roland.

In all of my gratitude for employment not ending, I wonder about and pray for all those people who contract serious illness and whose employers cannot keep them on the payroll. Undoubtedly, this would heap more worry and anguish on top of the horrible illness itself that we were fortunate to escape.

A new acquaintance who had GBS 10 years ago, stopped by to visit Roland, compare stories, and provide hope for all of us. We are so thankful for these GBS survivor visits. *God, remind us to be so helpful to those in need once we are able!*

Saturday, December 4, 1999

Another slow day for Roland but with happy visits from Karen, Emily, and Chad.

I spent the day at home cleaning and packing some of the essentials to move with us to the apartment. It hits me as I do this how little we truly need to live well. We possess so much extraneous "stuff," and I feel a sense of disappointment and shame that I have never noticed this before. How often we think we need more and then more on top of that, on and on over the years. I can't wait to see how little we will really need in the apartment.

Babysat Emily tonight. Home by 11:30 p.m.

Sunday, December 5, 1999

We can't believe it is early December, and we are able to sit outside in the garden a while! Another slow day therapy-wise. I missed the 2:50 p.m. shuttle, so I was delayed getting home to do more packing.

Chad and Dennis spent most of the day building a ramp so we can drive the electric wheelchair up into the back of Roland's small pick-up. Another blessing.

Monday, December 6, 1999

Therapy is back on normal schedule today. I see Roland really pushing hard thinking he'll be pretty much on his own soon and wanting to become as strong as possible *fast*.

I packed up the kitchen dishes, food, appliances, pots, pans, etc. Chad and Dennis continued working on the ramp and built a platform on which to set the portable toilet for easier transition from the wheelchair (Roland's idea conceived in those times alone at night).

Tuesday, December 7, 1999

The electric wheelchair arrived today. We spent most of therapy time learning how to use it. Roland can only use his head on the headrest to make it turn right, left, and go forward. He puffs into a tube to back up the chair. There are also remote controls I can use, and I'll need to remember to charge the chair battery every few days. It is a very intimidating piece of equipment! Using the remote controls, I ran the chair into a few walls and pieces of furniture while getting the hang of it (Roland wasn't in it while I practiced, and I didn't run down any people!). We all laughed, but inside I'm feeling overwhelmed and frightened about what lies ahead for us.

Wednesday, December 8, 1999

I moved all our boxes, clothes, and anything I could manage alone into our clean, very comfortable-looking apartment. The wood-burning fireplace looks promising for comfort during the cold winter months ahead. Chad, Dennis, Karen, Emily, and two good friends moved a couch, two chairs, the dining room table with six chairs, the TV and stand, two small tables, a twin bed, and a night stand. A hospital bed was delivered and set up for Roland. Two women friends helped me unpack the kitchen items and put them into cabinets. They also brought a wonderful soup luncheon for all to share.

I went home to sleep feeling tired, grateful, and full of happy anticipation for the homecoming tomorrow. All I can muster up to say to God tonight is, *"Thank You!"*

Thursday, December 9, 1999—Homecoming!

I took the last few needed items to the apartment and then went to the Department of Motor Vehicles to pick up the handicapped tag for the car. When I told the employee I needed a temporary handicapped car tag, she looked at the doctor's prescription and said, "This isn't temporary; it's permanent with renewal after five years." I think I hid the tears in my eyes and the lump in my throat from all those around me as I fought down the panic rising inside me. *Permanent?! Oh, no!*

I arrived at the hospital about 12:30 p.m. and began packing up all the clothes and various other 3½ months' accumulation of stuff as Roland went through the various, routine check-out procedures. It was wonderful receiving all the good wishes from the nurses and staff who have been so wonderful to us during our stay here. Roland took a solo run in the chair to return something to OT. As he left, his therapists gave him a hug, and all of the therapists stopped their tasks, walked over, and applauded as he rolled out of the room. He felt encouraged but also felt that conflict between wanting to go home and wanting to stay in that zone of support. AND, "Nurse Ratchett" came in to say goodbye, give her good wishes, and SMILED!

We happily maneuvered Roland in the wheelchair and all our plunder downstairs to the front door by 3:30 p.m. to meet Dennis and Chad bringing the new ramp. When they arrived, we carefully loaded Roland and baggage into our little truck. We then positioned the ramp and by remote control tried to send the wheelchair up the ramp into the truck bed. Alas! It would only go a little way and stop. None of our efforts succeeded in getting it to move all the way up into the truck bed. A hospital employee came by and informed us that the angle of the ramp was too steep and would never successfully allow the chair to move up into the truck. Many others hurriedly passed us by with quick, pitying glances but no offers of assistance. I'm quivering inside again! Please don't start crying NOW!

Just as we were standing there in the cold, dwindling daylight trying to think what to do next with this very heavy wheelchair, the strong son-in-law of Roland's roommate came by, saw the situation, and said, "Come on, we'll all just lift the chair into the truck." And so we did. Another set of helping hands lifting us up just as despair was beginning to descend upon us.

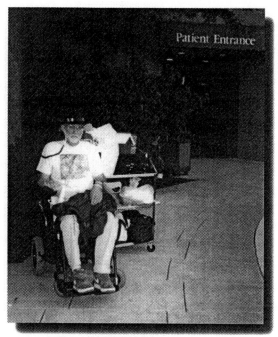

In his "Happy Hat," a going-home gift from a friend, Roland waits with his cart of "stuff" for the truck to take him "home" to the apartment.

Our family gathered at the new home for dinner brought to us by dear friends. Roland is pleased with the apartment and so happy to be home. He has trouble with the wheelchair wheels turning on the carpet, so we'll need to have the torque adjusted. We also discover that there is not room in the master bath to get the chair close enough to the shower chair for the transfer. Also, a small step-up at the front door will require a small ramp so the chair can enter the apartment. I'm not sure this "handicapped accessible" apartment was truly designed for the use of a wheelchair-bound person. But, we will adapt and do the best we can.

Chad stayed with us until about 10:00 p.m., helping us prepare Roland for bed and settle him comfortably. We are both happily exhausted.

Friday, December 10, 1999

I stagger out of bed around 7:30 a.m., remembering the quote from *Wizard of Oz*, but I'm saying, "Regina, this isn't hospital life anymore!"

Last night was rough. Roland needed the urinal several times during the night. So it seemed just as I got back to sleep, I would hear, "Reg, Reg, Honey, I need the urinal." He obviously didn't sleep well either and was cold. So during the night, I located my knit hat that helped keep his head warm. The sheets and blankets also hurt his feet.

A home care service has been contracted to provide an aide two hours in the morning to feed, bathe, and dress Roland. She arrived at 9:00 this morning. We found the second bathroom worked better for showering. With significant maneuvering, the chair could be positioned close enough to the tub for the transfer. During this two-hour break, I showered, had breakfast, and enjoyed a cup of coffee in solitude, gathering my strength for the coming day.

The at-home occupational and physical therapists stopped by for introductions and to determine plans for therapy. The wheelchair technician came and adjusted the chair so it works better now. A collapsible wheelchair that I could lift into the car or truck was delivered for use when we must go out.

Saturday, December 11, 1999

Sleep was restless and frequently interrupted last night. I hadn't envisioned nighttime being so unrestful and hope I can get through this. It has to get better; doesn't it? Sometimes the surprising thought creeps in that hospital life was better than this! I'm thankful I took early job retirement last year even though I had no idea this illness was looming before us. I never could have worked and kept up this strength-sapping caregiving. How do others do it?! *God please give them strength and mercy.*

Roland is stuck with only nurse Regina, as outside services are not provided on weekends. It took us most of the morning to get him up onto the toilet, dressed, and into the wheelchair. Then after I fed him, he spent some time at the table, stick in his mouth, turning the pages of the newspaper.

Tonight, with lots of manly assistance, we attended our friends' traditional pre-Christmas dinner. Chad came over to help load Roland into the wheelchair and then into the truck. Our friends placed a ramp up to their house and assisted me in getting Roland both out of and back into the truck. I assured them that we could manage unloading by ourselves at home—our first independent effort in this regard, and it would be in the dark and the cold. At the apartment complex, the curb cutout for wheelchairs is at the opposite end of the building from our apartment. So I must pull up to the cutout, unload the chair, transfer Roland into it, push him down the long sidewalk to our apartment, settle him in, return to the truck, and park in a designated space. It is so cold tonight. I'm getting grumpy. It's Christmas, and everyone else is so jolly. I want our old life back. I naively thought when I promised "in sickness and in health" in our marriage vows that it probably just meant putting up with his occasional cold—ha ha ha!

We had a wonderful time with our friends. However, after the hour-long procedure of getting Roland into bed, I am overcome with the powerful feeling of self-pity. I can't let him see this. I've got to be at least half as brave as he's been. *God, are You still here? I'm not doing so well. I'm beginning to be whiney. Please help me!*

Sunday, December 12, 1999

Roland really wanted to go to church today, and so did I. So, we got up at 6:30 after a sleep-fragmented night and arrived at church for the 11:00 a.m. service. It took us four hours just to get ready! Karen came by. She and friends helped load and unload at church. Everyone was so glad to welcome us back, and we were ever-so-thankful to be there.

The outing totally wore us both out, so it was early to bed. We cut down the time it took to 45 minutes!

Here I must vent about some of my feelings. People at church were so happy to see Roland and swamped him with, "How are you?" and "So glad to see you!" This made me happy, but I noticed no one asked how I was holding up. Some practically knocked me over getting to him. What am I—chopped liver? My suffering has been great, too. I don't necessarily want attention, but I was hurt by this. Yet, I feel guilty about feeling this way! I'll try to remember my feelings in the future when I'm inquiring about someone who is ill *and not forget their care-giver.*

Note to Readers:

Sunday, December 12, was the last day I could keep up a consecutive daily diary of events. When we got home, I became the nursing staff of one with a 24-hour shift, seven days a week—week after week after week. So the diary entry dates henceforth are sporadic. At the end, I will try to summarize my overall feelings during this time at home. I'm afraid I will never be able to convey adequately how difficult it was and how unprepared and inept I felt most of the time. My physical health suffered, but my spiritual health grew deeper and wider, for which I will ever be grateful.

Friday, December 17, 1999

Sherry, Tom, and Jesse flew here today to spend Christmas with us. It is so wonderful to have them here! They arrived after I had Roland in bed so Jesse was rather cautious about approaching the guy in bed wearing a stocking cap! They can be here until December 28. Another blessing: Four of my former work colleagues, who still get together with me once a month for dinner, decided against exchanging Christmas gifts this year. Instead, they ordered a large box of all kinds of food items (from ham to candies) for us to enjoy and to ease food planning and preparation. Again, I cry with humble thanksgiving.

Sunday, December 19, 1999

We all attended church as a family. We stopped by our Sunday School class, Trying Christians, as it was ending. It was Roland's first time in class since June. During the worship service, Roland found he could move his legs joyfully in time with our singing "Go, Tell it on the Mountain!"

Friday, December 24, 1999

With the help of Karen and Sherry, Roland was able to keep up an annual Christmas ritual. The girls bundled him up and took him to Main Street, where he liked to go on Christmas Eve to do some last-minute shopping but more simply to feel a bit of community Christmas spirit. It was bitingly cold, but they pushed him down the length of Main Street, from Newark United Methodist Church to Bing's Bakery and back, nearly a mile in all. They hit his favorite stores on Main Street: National 5 & 10, Agway, and Bing's. They had a good laugh making the transfers and fitting all three of them into the cab of his small pickup. He returned home chilled through and through but so happy. Thank you, daughters!

Christmas Day, December 25, 1999

Today we were blessed as all of our family gathered at Karen and Dennis' home. We had a wonderful Christmas dinner and basked in delight as we watched Jesse and Emily enjoy their Christmas surprises. The greatest gift for all of us was to be together, as tired, broken, and yet grateful, as we were. The spiritual gift of gratitude didn't come to me wrapped up with a pretty bow today. It came over these last four months as I learned of and confirmed beyond any doubt God's faithfulness. We've come through "the miry bog" (Psalm 40), but God has kept us secure.

Nap time for the girls rolled around in early afternoon, and we all decided to nap contentedly as well.

After an hour's slumber, I awoke itching with numerous hives on my body. I tried desperately not to scratch, but it was impossible, thus making them worse. I applied a liquid analgesic and took the pill form as well. Not too much relief. A call to the on-call doctor resulted in the pharmacy providing medicine.

During the night, when I got up to help Roland with the urinal, I felt dizzy and nauseated, and I slumped to the floor at his bedside. He lay there, helplessly, not able to see me, and knowing there was nothing he could do—not even call for help. Finally, I was able to crawl back to my bed and pull myself up to a standing position, empty the urinal, climb back into bed, and sink into slumber. I don't know if Roland needed me again that night. If so, he suffered in silence.

Sunday, December 26, 1999

Early in the morning, I awoke and stumbled into the bathroom, flipped on the light, and looked, horrified, at myself in the mirror. Big welts were scattered across my face, and one eye was swollen shut. My neck was red, and I itched all over. I knew on the other side of the door the man I love lay helplessly looking toward the closed door and crying silently that he could do nothing to help me.

I grabbed hold of the sink, looked into my one good eye, and said to my sorry self in a low, firm voice, "*Get a grip on yourself. God has brought you this far. He won't leave you now! You can't run away from this. Now, clean yourself up, open the door, and go into the day trusting and with no fear or pity."*

Somehow, I went on. The hives subsided gradually, and I tried to stay strong. I want to be full of strength and optimism. I have a hard time admitting to others that I feel weak, worn out, and in need of help. I hope I can improve in this area!

Early January, 2000

During the first few days home we tried to continue having Roland use the urinal during the night as well as during the day. The plan worked fine in the hospital where the night-duty nurses were awake and on the job. However, this caused exhausting, interrupted nights for me, and it began to take its toll.

It was suggested we purchase the "Texas Condom" type catheter. So, I bought a huge supply thinking this would solve our problem. However, they proved to pop off and spill urine all over Roland and the bed sheets. This did not help my rest or my mood.

Our church's parish nurse, ever the source of good advice since Roland's first days of GBS, told us about another, more complicated type of condom with a tube draining from the tip of the condom into a urinal-type of bag, which I hung on the side of his bed. She brought us a few of the condoms to try and told us where we could purchase more of them. This proved to be successful and helped us both to get the sleep we so desperately needed. Many thanks to this loving person for suggesting this solution and for her many supportive visits during these frustrating days. She always asked how I was doing and was sincerely concerned about how I was coping. Hope and peace once again edged out frustration and fatigue.

During this time, Roland continued to suffer discomfort on his feet from the sheets. It was hard for me to understand how only a lightweight sheet could cause so much pain, but he insisted the pain was great, as if the skin were broken or raw. He was not just imagining it. Yet he had to keep his feet and body warm. So he designed a solution in his mind and described to Chad what he needed from our house. Chad brought the boards with holes pre-drilled as requested, hammer, and nails. With Roland's coaching, Chad constructed a frame to place over the bed, covering Roland's body from the neck down. To our hour long nightly procedure of getting him settled in bed, I now added installing part of the frame and draping a sheet and electric blanket over the frame to create a space where he could be warm but have his feet untouched by the bedding. He also still needed to wear a stocking cap at night to keep his head warm. An interesting sight he made!

This is proving to be a very *rainy* winter. We don't go out unless Roland has a doctor's appointment. We notice that it rains on most of these days. It is very difficult to run out, pull the car up to the curb, run back in to load him into the chair and cover him up, and push him quickly out to the car in these downpours. Then, with the sliding board getting wet, I must slide him into the car, buckle him in, fold up the chair, and shove it into the trunk (or back of the truck)—all without getting completely drenched (and grumpy). We can't help but get pretty well soaked and chilled. Most of the time I feel pretty sorry for myself—and him too.

The very first doctor's appointment we had was on a day of extremely heavy downpours. It was necessary we make the trip because Roland hadn't seen the doctor since leaving the hospital. His feet were looking a bit strange (turning purple and spotted), and we had many questions and concerns.

Just as we were ready to leave, a friend arrived to help us load up. He had come from work during his lunch hour. We were so appreciative and were sorry he got so soaked, too. I am convinced his hands were God's hands today.

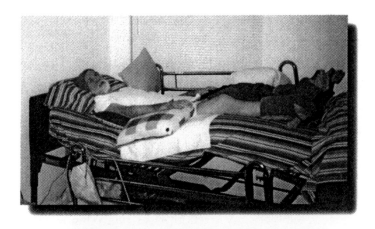

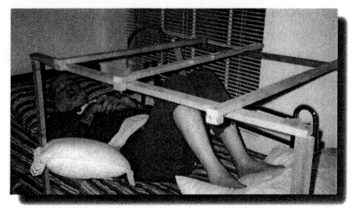

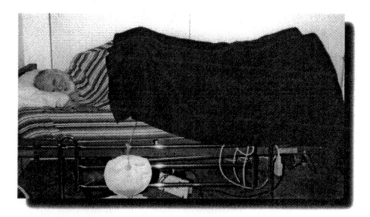

Ready for bed in one hour's time!

Coming out of the doctor's office, we repeated our soaking and again at home getting from the car into the apartment. As we approached the front door, I noticed a plastic bag hanging from the door knob. Inside, with wet hair in my eyes and my body chilled by wet clothing, I opened the bag to find homemade sticky buns lovingly made and delivered by a friend, in spite of the horrible weather. We both wept happy tears as I dried us off, changed us into dry clothes, made hot tea, and warmed the sticky buns. We ate in silent, humble gratitude, greatly comforted. I have never felt God's presence more fully than I did in partaking of this sweet nourishment with my sweetheart as rain pounded the windows. *We are okay; we are okay.* We are indeed safe in God's love.

All of today's events and all of the people who helped us make me think of candles—candles lighting up the darkness of the day. Indeed, these candles have lighted up many a dark day these last few months. I'm left speechless trying to take in God's magnificence and love.

January 24, 2000

We have morning aides three days a week now. Roland has physical therapy for an hour each Monday, Wednesday, and Friday and occupational therapy for an hour each Tuesday and Thursday here in the apartment. What a milestone! Lifted up and out of his wheelchair, Roland was able to take halting steps across the living room with the therapist holding him up on one side and Chad on the other. A new leg brace on his right foot and leg (called a MAFO) provides some helpful support. Roland was exhausted afterwards, but his eyes shone with happiness! Karen flashed the news by email to a wide circle of friends at work and elsewhere.

January 28, 2000

Roland moved his left arm and picked up half of a sandwich with thumb and index finger, lifted it toward his mouth while bending his head down to meet it, took a bite, and lowered his hand back down! What a great day! Again, an example of a small act being a monumental happy, celebratory moment. As I eat, I remember to be grateful that I can

feed myself, as well as do all the other bodily actions that were totally lost to Roland and are only so slowly, excruciatingly slowly, beginning to come back to him.

February 2, 2000

Today Roland lifted the phone receiver with his hand and called Karen's office by using the mouth stick to dial the numbers.

February 9, 2000

Roland now has a MAFO for the left leg also. A new piece of equipment was introduced

Roland feeding himself.
Oh, happy day!

today—a walker with arm straps that hold Roland's arms securely onto

forearm supports. He made one halting and shaky trip across the room and back to his chair, collapsing in joy!

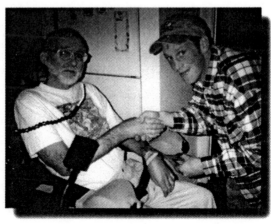

Chad cutting off Roland's
hospital ID bracelet in the
apartment

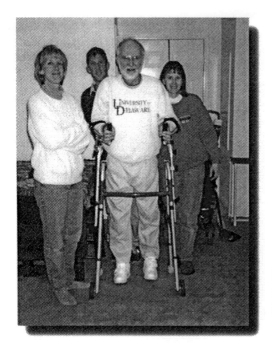

Walker with arm straps and lots of encouragement from children Karen, Chad, and Sherry

February 10, 2000

Today's main event was going to the doctor to check on Roland's feet, which are turning deep purple and are painful with a few really sore spots. The doctor called a doctor in Philadelphia (who also had GBS) for advice. Two specially prepared medications to improve circulation in his feet were recommended for which we have to go to a special pharmacy in a nearby town.

We made several trips to other specialists over the next few weeks. Without their knowledge and intervention, Roland would have come very near to having gangrenous feet. We are so grateful this "on-top-of-everything else" problem responded to treatment. The doctors and therapists are so quick to try to answer any question we have and to solve any problems promptly. The feet gradually returned to near normal condition. [Five years later: one very tender spot remains on one foot, but the color is good and circulation is better.]

Chad bringing me flowers from Roland on Valentine's Day. The sign reads, R+R=KSC

February 14, 2000

I ordered an Italian dinner "to go" for our Valentine's dinner tonight from a nearby restaurant. A love feast, though I fed him—and myself. It was delicious. Though we didn't exchange gifts, we recounted the many, many gifts in our lives. Our love is strong and sweet today, slightly beaten up but stronger than ever.

February 23, 2000

Roland was able to eat his entire lunch—sandwich, carrot sticks, chips—with his left hand with no help from me. A wrist brace helped. He still needs assistance with his beverages. He was able to walk six living room laps on his walker with a friend and me on each side holding his pants waistband!

February 24, 2000

First time today to use the regular toilet instead of the bedside one. He slid onto the sliding board from his chair onto the toilet. He is as proud as a newly potty-trained child. I'm so happy to be able to just flush the toilet and not have to clean out the "chamber-pot"! A friend gave me a gift certificate for a massage—a very much appreciated gift indeed!

March 1, 2000

Roland can rise up on one elbow on the bed almost up to a sitting position. I had to help him at the last to get completely up. He can now operate the TV remote control with left hand fingers. How he has missed that TV remote! How I liked having total control of the remote!

March 3, 2000

Pushed all the way up from lying on his side to sitting position today. Stood up out of wheelchair and, with me holding him under his arms, he was able to turn and collapse onto the bed. All these new feats leave him trembling with fatigue and happiness.

March 7 to March 31, 2000

Over this time period these are Roland's new accomplishments:

Blew his own nose

Bench-pressed a broom stick while lying on the bed

While lying on the bed on his back, pulled his slacks on

In the bed on his stomach, got up on all fours as though ready to crawl

At-home physical and occupational therapy as well as aide assistance ended, and our going out to a physical therapy facility began. Loading him into and out of the car is more routine now but still difficult in poor weather. Taking him to physical therapy, helping him out of the car and into the building, helping him out of his coat, and returning in a few hours to repeat it all backwards reminds me of my days with small children going to pre-school!

April, 2000

The new tasks Roland could accomplish by the end of this month are:

Brushing his teeth without my help

Washing his hands

Using a regular walker without arm supports

Using the urinal by himself (hooray, hooray!)

Can stand from chair and turn to sit in the car instead of using the sliding board

Can stand from bed or chair with me "spotting" him only and not lifting

On April 16, we held a "thank you" reception for the many, many wonderful people who helped us out in so many ways throughout this whole ordeal. Over 100 people attended and witnessed Roland take a short "victory lap" with his walker in front of the crowd with former therapists on each side of him but not holding him up. Many a happy, grateful tear was shed.

During April we found a ranch house for sale and bought it! It is smaller than our former home but is wheelchair accessible and perfect for us at this stage of our lives. We will be able to move into it in early June. We are thrilled! I try not to panic at the thought of cleaning out our home of 23 years, sorting and packing our belongings, moving all I can by myself, and again calling on dear friends to help us once more. Asking others for help has never been easy for me to do, and I'm still not comfortable asking even after this experience.

Brothers, who are friends of Chad, offer to buy our house and can settle on it in late July. We accept. This allows us to rent the apartment through June and gradually move into the new house during June, leaving July to finish moving out of our house and cleaning it up for the new owners. *Can I do all this?* Roland can't help me with all these moves. I have faith that since we've come this far with God's grace, the moves, too, will be accomplished!

May, 2000

More nerve recovery progress occurred this month allowing Roland to be able to do the following:

Better control in lifting one pound weights off the bed and over his head without dropping them

Walking around interior of apartment on walker with only a spotter

Pushed his wheelchair backward with his feet into therapy instead of *being* pushed

Stood (with his walker) normally at the toilet

Said goodbye to the electric wheelchair as he didn't need to rent it
anymore (We have purchased the small wheelchair.)

On May 23, we learned both Karen and Sherry are expecting their
second babies in January! On May 25, Karen suffered a miscarriage.
Great disappointment to us all. We enjoyed a visit with Roland's
brother and wife from Tennessee. We all were able to visit Longwood
Gardens thanks to our little portable wheelchair!

*Goodbye to electric
wheelchair! (A fond
thank you to the
technician who took it
away.)*

June, 2000

Highlights of this month include settlement on our new house on
June 2. Every day thereafter, after I drove Roland to therapy, I took
loaded boxes from the apartment to the new house and unloaded
them. I also spent part of most days at the old house packing up boxes
there, carrying them to the new house, and unpacking.

One morning a friend helped me wrap and pack dishes and other
breakables. I became really good at letting things go either to Goodwill

or be thrown out if they weren't in useable condition. It was a most satisfying clean sweep! All this packing, moving, unpacking, and tending to Roland's needs really wore me out. During this time my body became very achy, and my hips hurt terribly with any walking. I began walking with a limping, swaying motion. I ignored it and took aspirin to try to minimize the pain. I think I have gained weight these last few months as I tend to eat and snack more when I am under stress. I've not had time for much exercise other than whipping that wheelchair around!

Roland's progress continues. He can do a lot of his own grooming now, which pleases him and is a great time relief for me!

On the night of June 4, Roland didn't wear the catheter to bed. He was able to get out of bed, into the wheelchair and into the bathroom to use the urinal. He got up at 5:30 a.m., moved himself into his chair, opened the door, and wheeled down the ramp and back up with the morning paper. He is as proud as a child who might have done the same thing for the first time. Life is *almost* normal again! Hallelujah!

We totally moved into our new house on June 13 with many people giving of their time, talents and muscles once again. A new chapter begins!

Our winter is beginning to turn into spring—Thanks be to God!

Epilogue

2005

I think I quit keeping a daily journal after we moved because I was tired of thinking only of illness and all our limitations. I wanted a new start, in our new home, in a new neighborhood with new friends to make, to enlarge our community!

Roland's nerves have continued to slowly re-grow and are still improving. He has progressed from total and complete dependence upon me, and others, to being able again to work full-time, drive long distances, dig holes to plant trees, mow the yard, grow a beautiful garden *and* weed it, and just be a typical 62-year-old. He still occasionally returns to PT when he feels he needs more work on balance or hand and shoulder therapy. He still has frequent bouts of debilitating fatigue if he pushes too hard for a couple of days, numbness or tingling in limbs, isolated burning sensations on his feet, a halting-type gait, some distorted fingers, weak pinch and finger control, and muscles that don't always cooperate causing him to wobble and occasionally fall down. He still hopes someday to get his calves strong enough to lift his heels off the ground for the first time since September 1, 1999. We live in a state of thankfulness, however, instead of complaint. We know that some GBS victims have more serious and long-lasting effects with recovery lasting a lifetime.

We are very thankful for our insurance company, Blue Cross and Blue Shield of Delaware, for paying most of our staggering bills. Without insurance, we would be deeply in debt as well as having our lifetime savings wiped out. I'm deeply grieved to think a person could possibly suffer GBS and not have health insurance—indeed a nightmare situation as with any other major health disaster when there is no insurance.

Our deepest thanks and gratitude go to the many, many people who physically carried us through this ordeal—from doctors to the friend delivering sticky buns on a rainy day. And we express thanks and awe for all who prayed for us along the way—from the orderly on the first day to friends and friends of friends all over the country who heard of our plight and to our little granddaughters' pleas to God for their grandfather. How magnificent are the hearts and hands of God's angels! And, of course, our deepest gratitude is to God for never ever leaving our sides and for picking us up after every stumble and fall, for listening to and understanding our fears and uncertainties, walking beside us all the way, in the light and in the dark—a very present help in our time of trouble.

My wish for all of you is that you have no fear as you walk the dark valleys of life. God will not forsake you. Look—and find the candles. I hope, too, that we all may be part of that wonderful, helpful "community" to those who suffer. Never underestimate the power of a prayer, a "thinking-of-you" card, or a half-dozen warm sticky buns.

How can I sum up all that I've learned from a hard life experience? I now try to remember to look for the good in whatever is happening, no matter how awful or traumatic the situation. In every grueling day, there was some comfort or something good about it somewhere. I think we must look hard for the good. It's not always readily apparent and may not be recognized until much later.

I hope I've learned gratitude—gratitude to God for everything from medical progress to just being able to lift a fork, to scratch my nose, and to clip my own toenails. How magnificent is the working of our bodies, our minds, our hearts! (Roland says the miracles are that our bodies work most of the time and that we do not get sick more often, not just that sometimes we recover from really bad things.) Miracles do abound!

Here are a few of the things Roland says he learned from having GBS, and I would like to share them with you:

- It's a way to lose 35 lbs. in a month.
- Some of the stuff that seemed very important before: it wasn't.
- There are a bunch of good people willing to help a friend.
- Patience is a good thing to have if you are paralyzed.
- Physical fitness is a good thing to have BEFORE you get ill or need physical rehab; it helps later.
- I now identify with infants and toddlers learning to use new muscles.
- Nurses, aides, and therapists work hard, and I would not want to be one.
- Be as congenial as possible to nurses and aides; you may not have to wait so long for a bedpan.
- The best decision I ever made was to ask Regina to marry me.
- Not everyone knows that applesauce is an essential food that must be mixed with each bite of meat, potatoes, etc.

And last, what was once merely my spoken "belief" that God will never leave our side has become an actual experience of feeling and knowing undoubtedly that is true. It is one thing to espouse a belief and another to hang on to that belief when the going gets rough. No matter what the future holds for us, I know God will never forsake us. My deepest hope and prayer is that this discovery (or confirmation) will come to all who read this diary. May our experience give you comfort, encouragement, and strength in life's dark valleys. Trust in God's promises. God's unfailing love is the candle of light and hope in any darkness.

"For I am sure that neither death, nor life, nor angels, nor principalities, nor things present, nor things to come, nor powers, nor height, nor depth, nor anything else in all creation, will be able to separate us from the love of God in Christ Jesus our Lord."

—*Romans 8:38-39*

Bible Comfort

Here are a few other Scriptures I found during this challenge and continue to find comforting and sustaining:

Joshua 1:9—Have I not commanded you? Be strong and of good courage; be not frightened, neither be dismayed; for the Lord your God is with you wherever you go.

Psalm 23—The Lord is my shepherd, I shall not want; he makes me lie down in green pastures. He leads me beside still waters; he restores my soul. He leads me in paths of righteousness for his name's sake. Even though I walk through the valley of the shadow of death, I fear no evil; for thou art with me; thy rod and thy staff, they comfort me. Thou preparest a table before me in the presence of my enemies; thou anointest my head with oil, my cup overflows. Surely goodness and mercy shall follow me all the days of my life; and I shall dwell in the house of the Lord for ever.

Psalm 27:1, 13-14—The Lord is my light and my salvation; whom shall I fear? The Lord is the stronghold of my life; of whom shall I be afraid?

I believe that I shall see the goodness of the Lord in the land of the living! Wait for the Lord; be strong; and let your heart take courage; yea, wait for the Lord!

Psalm 40 (the whole chapter), 1-3 only here—I waited patiently for the Lord; he inclined to me and heard my cry. He drew me up from the desolate pit, out of the miry bog, and set my feet upon a rock, making my steps secure. He put a new song in my mouth, a song of praise to our God. Many will see and fear, and put their trust in the Lord.

Psalm 46:1—God is our refuge and strength, a very present help in trouble.

Psalm 91:3-6—For he will deliver you from the snare of the fowler and from the deadly pestilence; he will cover you with his pinions, and under his wings you will find refuge; his faithfulness is a shield and buckler. You will not fear the terror of the night, nor the arrow that flies by day, nor the pestilence that stalks in darkness, nor the destruction that wastes at noonday.

Psalm 121 (most encouraging to me)—I lift up my eyes to the hills, from whence does my help come? My help comes from the Lord, who made heaven and earth. He will not let your foot be moved, he who keeps you will not slumber. Behold, he who keeps Israel will neither slumber nor sleep. The Lord is your keeper; the Lord is your shade on your right hand. The sun shall not smite you by day, nor the moon by night. The Lord will keep you from all evil; he will keep your life. The Lord will keep your going out and your coming in from this time forth and for evermore.

Isaiah 40:31—but they who wait for the Lord shall renew their strength, they shall mount up with wings like eagles, they shall run and not be weary, they shall walk and not faint.

Isaiah 43:2-3—When you pass through the waters I will be with you; and through the rivers, they shall not overwhelm you; when you walk through fire you shall not be burned, and the flame shall not consume you. For I am the Lord your God, the Holy One of Israel, your Savior.

Jeremiah 17:7-8—Blessed is the man who trusts in the Lord, whose trust is the Lord. He is like a tree planted by water, that sends out its roots by the stream, and does not fear when heat comes, for its leaves remain green, and is not anxious in the year of drought, for it does not cease to bear fruit.

Jeremiah 29:13-14—You will seek me and find me; when you seek me with all your heart, I will be found by you, says the Lord. . . .

Matthew 11:28—Come to me, all who labor and are heavy-laden, and I will give you rest.

Matthew 28:19-20—Go therefore and make disciples of all nations, baptizing them in the name of the Father and of the Son and of the Holy Spirit, teaching them to observe all that I have commanded you; and lo, I am with you always, to the close of the age.

2 Corinthians 1:3-5—Blessed be the God and Father of our Lord Jesus Christ, the Father of mercies and God of all comfort, who comforts us in all our affliction, so that we may be able to comfort those who are in any affliction, with the comfort with which we ourselves are comforted by God. For as we share abundantly in Christ's sufferings, so through Christ we share abundantly in comfort too.

2 Corinthians 4: 6-10 (7-8 here)—But we have this treasure in earthen vessels, to show that the transcendent power belongs to God and not to us. We are afflicted in every way, but not crushed; perplexed, but not driven to despair; persecuted, but not forsaken; struck down, but not destroyed; always carrying in the body the death of Jesus, so that the life of Jesus may also be manifested in our bodies.

And may we all live each day of our lives remembering *Matthew 5: 14-16*—You are the light of the world. A city set on a hill cannot be hid. Nor do men light a lamp and put it under a bushel, but on a stand, and it gives light to all in the house. Let your light so shine before men, that they may see your good works and give glory to your Father who is in heaven.

The Author

Regina R. Roth was born and raised in the wonderful town of Fayetteville, Arkansas. She met Roland, a native of Stuttgart, Arkansas, in 1961 at the Wesley Foundation, a United Methodist ministry on the University of Arkansas campus, where both were students. They married in 1964 at Central Methodist Church in Fayetteville. From 1965 to 1971, Champaign, Illinois, was home while Roland completed his graduate studies in zoology and where daughters Karen and Sherry were born. Since July 1971, they have lived in Newark, Delaware. There Roland taught and did research in wildlife conservation, ornithology, and other areas until his retirement in 2005. In Newark, Regina bore son Chad, served in various positions in Newark United Methodist Church, earned an M.Ed. in Secondary Counseling, and worked as a school guidance counselor for 19 years. She retired from Cecil County, Maryland Public Schools in 1998.

Besides their three children, Regina and Roland have been blessed with sons-in-law Dennis Aniunas and Tom Hershberger and five granddaughters—all of whom contribute to the strength and joy of their family.

Regina will donate proceeds after expenses from the sale of this book to neuro-muscular disease research. Regina and Roland welcome your questions and comments and can be reached at: rroth@udel.edu.

Regina and Roland Roth, May 9, 2005

LaVergne, TN USA
24 February 2011
217760LV00001B/230/A